M000113455

A CHANNELING HANDBOOK
BY CARLA L. RUECKERT

Other books by L/L Research:

Living the Law of One 101: The Choice
A Wanderer's Handbook
A Book of Days
Secrets Of The Ufo
The Ra Material (The Law Of One, Book One)
The Law Of One, Book Two
The Law Of One, Book Three
The Law Of One, Book Four
What Is Love?, a coloring book for kids
The Crucifixion Of Esmerelda Sweetwater, a parable for all ages, by
Don Elkins and Carla L. Rueckert

Portions of this book have appeared in somewhat different form in
Metapsychology; The Journal of Discarnate Intelligence.

ISBN: 0-945007-07-8

L/L Research
P.O. Box 5195
Louisville, KY 40205

E-mail: contact@llresearch.org
www.llresearch.org

PREFACE

Although the art and practice of channeling is at least as ancient as written history, and although a scholarly work of research comparing and contrasting various kinds of channeling throughout history would undoubtedly be fascinating, this volume is in no way intended as such a work. It is, rather, a workbook for the practicing channel, or for one who is contemplating the attempt to learn how to produce channeled material. It is my response to the veritable explosion of new channels, and especially to the many new-age weekends which teach the mechanics of channeling, which are very easy to master, but which do not give students a firm metaphysical basis for the appropriate use of this gift.

I became a channel in 1974 and have pursued that gift to this day. I have taught students the mechanics of channeling, but I hope that I have done a good deal more than that, for it has always been my intention to make available not only the how-tos of being an instrument but the whys. Channeling is not a parlor game. There can be emotional, mental and even physical difficulties which spring from the misuse of this practice. It is my hope that this volume will help those who wish to avoid such problems. The ideas which are offered herein are my opinion only. It is hoped that they will help you. If they do not, please leave them behind without a second thought.

I would like to acknowledge my enormous debt to several people, for although I was given the gift of faith and the temperament to sustain an effort which I thought well-begun, I would never have begun channeling were it not for the encouragement of Donald T. Elkins, my beloved friend, partner and companion of many years, who died in 1984. His faith in my gift far outmatched mine from the beginning, and his encouragement was equaled by the disciplined compassion of his counsel to me as I encountered situation after situation which had been unfamiliar to me previously.

James Allen McCarty has also encouraged and supported me in every imaginable way in the very humble service that I perform, and this book would have been physically impossible to create without his emotional support and the nimbleness of his and Kimberly Howard's fingers.

Thanks go also to my family and faithful friends and those many members of our meditation group over the years, without whose enquiring questions and hunger for truth there would have been no call generated for our contacts to answer; without whose personal love, encouragement, support and tolerance I would be poor indeed in the currency of shared love.

The most central and deep thanks I offer to my personal Lord and Savior, Jesus the Christ, whose promise of redemption and living Spirit sustain me every moment of my life, and to the community of Christ's own with whom I worship, Calvary Episcopal Church, Louisville, and to my spiritual director and priest, Father Ben Sanders, whose godly encouragement and censure alike have strengthened me.

Spring is creeping quietly into our inland hills, touching the burgeoning pussy-willow and unfurling our winter hearts to warm, free bloom. Peace to each of you from Kentucky.

Carla L. Rueckert
Louisville, Kentucky
February 10, 1987

To all, visible and invisible,
who seek to be channels
for love and light.

CARLA LISBETH RUECKERT

Carla Lisbeth Rueckert was born on July 16, 1943 in Lake Forest, IL. She grew up in Louisville, KY and graduated from the University of Louisville in 1966, earning a Bachelor of Arts Degree in English Literature. This was followed by a Master's degree in Library Arts from Spalding College in 1971. Carla worked as a librarian for a thirteen-grade school until she was hired away by Don Elkins to do paranormal research. They formally created L/L Research in 1970. Carla served as a vocal channel from 1974–2011,and was the instrument for The Law Of One series. During her lifetime Carla authored and channeled thirteen published books, channeled approximately 1,500 different transcripts, sustained volumes of written and spoken correspondence with spiritual seekers, wrote poetry, danced, gardened, and sang with a heart full of praise and thanksgiving, both in the small moments of home life and in the church choir her entire life. Carla loved Jesus, loved serving, loved seeking, and loved life itself. She married her soulmate, Jim McCarty, in 1987, and passed away at home during Holy Week on April 1, 2015.

Carla's life work continues through her non-profit organization, L/L Research. You can find all of her work available for free at www.llresearch.org.

Photo by Glenda Love Jaggers

Table Of Contents

Chapter One
What Is Channeling?

Channeling is the reproduction by words or sounds of concepts not generated within one's own conscious mind but transmitted from the subconscious mind or through the subconscious mind into the conscious mind from an impersonal or nonpersonal entity or principle. A good analogy to channeling would be the pipe which carries water. The pipe does not create the water, but rather receives it from a source external to its own identity. There are things a pipe or channel can be and do to enhance the delivery of pure channeling/water through itself: it can keep itself clean and free from corrosion; it can remove obstructions; it can strengthen its walls or enlarge its diameter; it can make new connections. However, the only control it has over the water it channels through itself is the care with which it has allowed itself to be connected; the only control a pipe has over the appropriateness of the position and place of efflux of this water is its care in positioning that opening. And of course, it must obey the mechanical rules of water distribution, which are quite simple, but inexorable.

People are designed to be channels, just as a pipe is designed to carry water. Indeed, in a sense, we all channel our lives moment by moment, thought by thought, relationship by relationship and experience by experience. Seldom is what we say, think and do completely under our conscious control. Almost always we are, to some extent, channeling unconscious thoughts. Any seminar which advertises that it can teach you to "get in touch with your psychic powers" is preparing for itself an extremely easy and potentially fruitful job—fruitful to the seminar holders financially perhaps, and personally almost surely; fruitful to the participants only to the extent of their own intuition and common sense and the tools that they have been given by their instructors. Since there is a gap between what common sense can tell you and what most instructors can express in a single seminar, the student must either learn further by making mistakes, as I did, or come across information such as this which is at least intended to bridge the gap.

There are too many kinds of channeling to mention. Perhaps the image which represents channeling to the average person is that of the spiritualist séance. In this practice, a medium sits with a group of people who wish to communicate with ghosts of one kind or another, relatives, Indian guides, spirit doctors, inner-plane masters, and so forth. This form of mediumship is not the kind of channeling about which I know much, and those who wish to learn to be spiritualistic mediums are advised to go to a Spiritualist church and inquire as to where the nearest center is that offers such a course of teaching. I note this, not because I have any disapproval of the practice, nor because I am unfamiliar with the practice of spiritualistic mediumship, but because it and other well-established and thorough schools of mediumship—the American Indian tradition and its medicine men and women are another good example—offer a perfectly adequate and perhaps somewhat specialized form of instruction to interested students. This book may be of help to one who is already under the instruction of a Spiritualist teacher or an American Indian medicine person, but it can never be a substitute for the support of the whole tradition.

Of course I don't pretend or expect that this volume can be a substitute for the on-going support of a teacher and a supporting group of other channels and students, but in a less structured line of channeling, the book does become far more helpful.

What other types of channeling are there then? The religious and traditional, for one. The prophets and some few saints in the Christian church were channels. The Old Testament is filled with the beauty of the prophets' words, most notably Isaiah's, whose words about the sacrificial lamb were so very prophetic of the Incarnation of Jesus the Christ. These holy men and women saw visions, heard voices. Moses, in fact, heard the words of the Lord straight out and merely reported on the conversation.

Then there are the new-age religions, and independent but vaguely Christian sources which channel archangels, various lesser angelic presences, spiritual masters of various kinds, such as Kuthumi, and of course, Jesus, under various names. In some of the best of this kind of channeling one is uplifted and one's feelings are elevated to a rarefied joy by the inspirational writing of the channel. The religious channel has an obvious bias, and consequently the message does not "get through" to everyone who happens to read the material. The Bible, for example, is the best-selling channeling of all time, but it does not appeal to every reader and many are the Bibles which carry far more dust than fingerprints. One of my friends recently read STARSEED TRANSMISSIONS, and tossed it aside without a second thought.

"Didn't you like the work?" I asked.

"I got absolutely nothing out of it," he replied.

For him the religious content so interfered with his ability to accept the material that all of the superstructure of concept and detail which had so inspired me served to shut his ears. One who desires to channel a religious presence, therefore, will need to come to terms with the fact that the bias of the material will block that material from many listeners and readers.

There is a large category of metaphysical channeling sources and an almost gaudy grab bag of extraterrestrial beings, ascended masters, principles, nature spirits, and uncategorizeable individuals. There are philosophers which offer general counsel as well as a fairly thorough philosophical system in which the counsel is seated which have, in addition to a fairly coherent philosophy and point of view, the willingness to offer rather extensive and personal information to individuals. The ascended masters are channeled by several large and organized groups of instruments, such as the Order of the Rosy Cross, Eckankar and Theosophists. Many a person has channeled Kuthumi; many an Astaran has discovered Zoser for himself, and so forth. The common theme of the inner-master channeling is the belief in the rightness of the proposition that there are some individuals who have, at some point in their life experience, gained access to great and hidden wisdom and who have, after death, chosen to remain both discarnate and available to those of us who seek the truth during our lives on Earth. This belief in a gnostical hierarchy of wisdom predicates that there be someone able to tell the truth-seeker how to find the gatekeeper of each door which unlocks the next layer or hierarchy of understanding, the next piece of wisdom which will, in the end, cause us to become masters ourselves. Most of these systems teach the channeling in a coherent and useable format, and I can only recommend to those who are interested in this kind of channeling that, as always, discrimination should be used, and those powers of discrimination honed carefully, for although one system may seem much like another, each comes with a dogma or doctrine with which it is necessary to be conversant and to accept, at least in some part, in order for the student's experience with the system to be satisfactory. Indeed, part of middle America, the lodge—Moose, Elk, Mason, Shriner—is a good example of this basic gnostic kind of channeling. I am not saying that your husband or father, boyfriend, or nephew is channeling when he goes to a Shriner's convention. However, those who structured these organizations were certainly channeling this type of "wisdom" information.

Perhaps the most famous of the metaphysical or philosophical channels is Edgar Cayce, whose channeling indicated that its source was the Akashic Record itself. Cayce's work has been especially interesting to researchers because of the completeness with which records were kept of sessions in which many evidential details were given which proved to be true and which produced a large number of healings. The accuracy of the healing channelings causes even the most scientifically oriented researcher to express at least some interest in the philosophical material that echoes through the healing material and takes up the center stage of the readings which were supported by those who paid to ask philosophical questions. Edgar Cayce is no longer incarnate, but the same Akashic Record claims now to be present again in the channeling of Awareness by Paul Shockley of the Aquarian Church of Universal Service in McMinnville, Oregon.

There are fairies, and yes, Tinker Bell, I will clap for you! Such are the musings of one who is seriously studying the work with nature spirits of medicine men and women in the American Indian tradition, fairy tale buffs and Findhorn, to name three sources. Findhorn's account of the contact with the plant devas and the subsequent growing of very large and healthy vegetables in the barren, sandy soil of the northern coast of Scotland is most impressive, and the American Indian tradition is also persuasive in its accounts of the relationship of sensitive Indian men and women with the spirits of their elk, eagle and so forth.

There is a large variety of purported UFO contactees. Phylos, Clarion, and George Hunt Williamson's channeling of Brother Philip all speak of, or are themselves, allegedly extraterrestrial contacts. There are many channels of a group calling itself the Federation of Planets, the Confederation of Planets or the Confederation of Planets in the Service of the Infinite Creator. I, myself, am one of those channels. Especially interesting is the channeling of Vinod and Probert of "The Nine" and the channeling, which was only possible by Uri Geller's presence, of Hoova.

Rather than attempting to be complete in any of these categories of channeling I shall dismiss that hopeless task with a shrug and a grin. You see, there are literally millions of people channeling on Earth today, channeling all kinds of entities. Far from such information being rare, it is almost unimaginably plentiful. I have personally channeled hundreds of thousands of words and seen millions more in others' transcripts and books. The activity is pervasive for a very simple reason: it is part of human nature. And, like any other thing that man can do, it is a thing that most predictably will continue to be done, sometimes poorly, sometimes exquisitely well.

CHAPTER TWO
WHY CHANNEL?

You can see that there is a plethora of channeled material available to the student, beginning with the most ancient Vedic holy work and reaching to the very latest wisdom from the world of the invisible, from whatever source. The information has, or tends to have, pervasively common themes such as the ascendancy of the rightness of peace between peoples and good will among nations, and the nearness in time of a planetary transformation. The typical content of such messages was covered in a book previously written by Donald T. Elkins and me in 1976, SECRETS OF THE UFO.

In addition, each body of channeled information usually contains some concepts peculiar to it, often in direct contradiction to other bodies of channeled material. Not only is the amount of this information staggering, but also enormously confusing, if one attempts to make every fact of even two instruments' channeled material fit into any kind of congruency.

There are many adherents of any orthodox body of channeled material, such as Jews and Christians, who would suggest that the truth has already been given. (No arguing here: if you do not think of your favorite holy work as having been channeled, you have thinking to do, not talking!) At the very least, people who have come to believe in the doctrine presented by a body of channeled material will be very puzzled about why in the world people would want to engage further in this activity of channeling when the truth is already known. In accepting one body of channeled material, many people come to feel that all other bodies of material are outlawed. This bias isolates the self from others and predicates the assumption that man can *know* something, not only for himself but also for others, in the world of faith. But we can not. Simple faith finds inspiration wherever its discrimination tells it that a spirit of truth dwells. My discrimination is not anyone else's, and what works for me, works for me alone. Nevertheless, those who believe in a doctrine, and rightness by literal fact, to be legislated for all, have always outnumbered those who feel that the truth is expressed in mystery through personal faith.

Moreover many, especially in the Christian tradition, feel that all latter-day channeling is Satanic in nature. There is scripture to support almost any point of view—Southerners before the war between the states used scripture to rationalize and support the practice of slavery—and it is not surprising that one may find scriptural passages both to commend the careful use of discernment of spirits and to condemn the same channeling as a mediumship which is punishable by death. The acceptance of either point of view without discriminating thought is not recommended; however, any student who wishes to explore the possibility of becoming a channel needs to reckon with the probable reaction of the very ones who love you the most: if they are fundamental Christians, and perhaps even if they are not, they will find such activity somewhat frightening, and may interpret what you are doing as a form of Satanic possession. If your desire to channel is strong enough to withstand others' bad opinions, fine. If you are potentially ready to lose a husband or a family, a friendship or a job, because of your desire to channel, then stop and think, perhaps you are on the track that you should be on. If you are serene and humble, your family will gradually relax. It is especially to be pointed out that those who do become channels and do encounter this reaction from those they love need to refrain from defending themselves, for it is totally unethical for a channel to present itself as a stumbling block in the way of another seeker's spiritual path. That's just not fair. *You* do not feel happy when you are criticized. Avoid criticizing others. If what you are doing is being done in the spirit of love, your words and your love will speak for themselves to most.

Many people who are reading this book are possessed by nothing more than curiosity about this very interesting phenomenon, channeling. There is nothing wrong with curiosity. It is commendable. I don't think that there is anything wrong with skimming the surface of a large variety of things, testing the waters, seeing what is for you and what is not. I can only suggest that in sampling the gift of channeling, you who are merely curious seek a controlled group situation in which you have a structured way of going about learning the mechanics of this gift's manifestation. Take the waters, in a short burst. It is centrally important, if you do not intend to persevere in the discipline of vocal or written channeling, that you go no further than will satisfy the curiosity, because any longer exposure will, if the contact is a poor one, tend to cause disintegration of your personality and your experience; if the contact is a good one, any longer exposure will bring about new understanding and, thereby, place you under the responsibility, which is that what one knows, one is responsible for reflecting in one's life.

Sue Leonard, a friend of mine who teaches Free Soul in Colorado, was talking to me on the phone the other day about people's seeming reliance on her when she was doing channeling. She asked her class, she said, whether, if they had a difficult financial decision to make, they would call ten people at random on the telephone and ask their opinions, without knowing whom they were calling. The class immediately recognized the folly of such a procedure. How, then, she asked them, could they consider her extra-special because she was a telephone? Rather severely, she suggested that they all stop gold-plating the telephone and start seeking their own inner senses of recognition which would be able to discriminate regarding new information.

If you do not want to change your life; if you do not wish to live the life in which channeling has its best environment, do not persist past satisfying of your curiosity in channeling. Stop immediately and go on to something else, for there is indeed a great "supermarket" in the realm of the psychic and occult, and metaphysical truth is sold in many packages these days, as it has always been. There is no penalty in skipping about from discipline to discipline. The penalty is for remaining in one discipline long enough to learn from it, and then not using this knowledge in the service of others.

It should be said here that I have a strong bias towards service to others. It is possible to channel in a negative sense, and there are negative entities and principles in the universe which are most delighted to make contact with a human channel. As in any positive channeling, this type of channeling has many subdivisions and teachers. However, my bias against negative information causes I me to refrain from describing sources of such information.

I come to channeling from the mystical Christian tradition. I was born a mystic and very probably had the gift of faith at birth. Consequently, my motivation for channeling was to be of service to others. Of those who are serious about channeling, this is an almost constant attitude. Regardless of how efficacious a person may be as an instrument, regardless of the relative beauty and inspirational value of the channeling, the motive of most instruments is the old white magical motto, "I desire to know in order to serve." A large number of human beings seem to be able to go through their lives asking nothing more than to have a peaceful and happy home life, enough money to buy what they need for themselves and their families and some gusto to grab. Others of us, for no clear reason, have a bug in our ear. Christian or not, mystics are convinced that we have some work to do in this lifetime; some feel that they came to Earth to accomplish some mission. When one weeds out the seriously neurotic or psychotic people who are deluding themselves first and others secondly, one still has a very large and pretty committed body of people who wish to be servants of humankind. Common beliefs among such people are that it is possible to push the envelope of mystery back a little further and still a little further so that the noumenal, though infinitely receding before us, can be to some slight extent asymptotically approached.

Another assumption is that the unseen overshadows the seen, has created the seen world, and is far more real than that which we see with our physical eyes and touch with our physical senses. The third assumption among mystics is that other people are worth serving, and that it is possible to serve them. These assumptions, put together, give to the student who wishes to be of service by channeling the feeling of reaching out to all of humanity as a shepherd would reach out to those sheep he so carefully tends and to whose care he is dedicated. It is clear from this image that one of the great dangers of deciding to channel is that one will become self-important. Instruments (another word for channel) are not an elite. An instrument knows no more than the person who hears the channeling. This is not only a truism; it is also true. We are all bozos on this bus. Remember the analogy of the pipe and the water. Instruments are pipes. Everything that they do, they do prior to receiving the water that flows through them. That which flows through them may well be from a higher source. The channels themselves, however, are sheep, except in the exaltation of the self by the One which overshadows it and speaks in the spirit of love and truth.

Would you believe that I know no less than three people—albeit slightly—who have channeled their own destiny as that of bearing the Christ child and being His mother in His second Earthly pilgrimage after two thousand years? It's true. No end of folly has been perpetrated by people who accept the falsehood that because they are channels they represent an elite and, in some way, have a leg up on the rest of humanity. Please examine your motives. If you are channeling for reasons other than curiosity or a desire to be of service to others and to the Creator, it would be well to avoid the practice of channeling, for, as I have said, it can really land one in the soup emotionally, mentally and even physically. There is the capacity in each of us to lose contact with waking reality as it is perceived by the bulk of humankind. The possibility of the disintegration of the waking personality is made far more probable as one opens the integrated personality to the incursion of deeply impersonal, often external personalities. Channeling's no joke. Why do you want to channel? Why are you channeling? Please use some discrimination!

The lack of discrimination can have heavy penalties, and perhaps an example or two would be in order. If you are channeling, and any of these seems somewhat familiar to you, you may be able to do a little work in this area and begin to experience a far more efficacious career as a channel.

Example one is a student I had in 1975. She was an intensely intellectual, likable sort of a person, approaching 30, prematurely middle-aged and dressed in that manner, and extremely swayed by whatever she was experiencing at the moment. Every time the L/L doors were open, Millie was there (not her real name). She began to try to channel on her own, and received information almost immediately. She was, for instance, one of the three "Virgin Mary's" of which I spoke. Later, she called me in a state of nervous excitement with the information that a presidential candidate was about to get onto an airplane which would crash, killing him. She wanted me to call a psychic (Jeanne Dixon, whom I didn't know) with this information so that she could warn the candidate. My attempts to explain to her why I was not going to fulfill her request were not comprehended, and she rang off convinced that I had turned against her. Not very long afterwards, a Catholic priest called us and told us that she had sought sanctuary in his church because she was being attacked by Satanic forces. She felt that her mother and father were possessed and she did not trust anyone except us. He wanted to know if we could come get her, because she had had nothing to eat for days and had refused even water for the 48 hours that she had spent in his church. Reluctantly we went and got Millie, brought her home, and attempted to feed her a light meal. It was after midnight. She was too tense even to lie down. When we suggested that she relax, she accused us of attempting to control her mind, and ran from the apartment before we could stop her. We went after her but could not find her since we lived close to a park with many winding, hilly roads and too many turns for us to be able to guess which way she had gone.

We notified her favorite professor, the priest who had called us, and her parents that she was loose in the city, clad in nightshirt only, driving a car that was almost dry of gas and penniless. It was all that we could think of to do. Millie ended up in triage at a mental hospital, where she was in therapy for some months. Upon her release from the hospital she brought the leaders of Ananda Marga, a spiritually oriented Buddhist sect, to see us. She wished to prove to them that we had evil thought-forms which were influencing our work and disturbing her. The orange-robed Ananda Marga teacher had a good deal of psychic ability, and a sense of humor as well. After demonstrating that he could tell us things that he could not possibly have known, thereby reaffirming to Millie his skill, he told her that we did not have any such presences about our benighted heads. "But they believe in magic," said Millie. The leader humorously picked up the remote control for our television. "So do I," he said. "Let me show you some magic." He pointed the device at our television and across the room it sprang into electronic life. "Magic," he said in his charmingly accented voice. "You see." Millie was not pleased. I am happy to say that she gradually got better.

I had scrupulously counseled Millie from the beginning, as I do all of my students, to avoid any thought of learning channeling on her own. This is not a pursuit to be undertaken in solitude. When she began anyway, I continued to counsel her against it. She interpreted my counselings as insults, feeling that I was attempting to "corner the market" and do all the channeling myself.

Example number two: A long-established channel whom I will call Susan wrote us after the first Law of One book came out, asking for advice on how to improve her meditation group. She had been teaching channeling to her students and, as always, she had succeeded in teaching this easily transmitted gift. (It is the improvement of quality in channeling that is the true gift and life-work, not the ability to learn the mechanics.) She had intended, she said, for these students to remain in the group. However, they were leaving the group and starting their own meditation and study groups. She wondered what she was doing wrong.

I really couldn't diagnose any problem from the information in her first letter, and wrote describing the way my meetings are run and the expectations I have of listening gladly to those who wish to share the responsibility and honor of being instruments with me. "I am so much happier to listen than to channel that I consider it a great boon to be able to enjoy other people's channeling," I wrote.

Her second letter was far more revealing. She had, she said, the hope not of listening to others' channeling, but of using other channels to confirm the virtue of what she had already channeled. When I wrote back suggesting that perhaps her ego was getting in the way, she became defensive and said that I was a very judgmental person. Not too long after that, she began getting large amounts of information having to do with the "terrible catastrophes" that are to come, suggesting that it would be well for the chosen ones who were listening to her words to band together in a remote area for survival purposes. The channeling even included suggestions as to the supplies needed, including diapers. Note the twist of "love and light" information into messages of doom and the movement from universal love to the establishment of an elite group, which then must defend itself against outsiders who do not belong.

I do not shrug off the channeled information concerning the coming transformation of our planet or ourselves; however, it seems to me that we who are aware of the possibility of such remarkable events, if we are functioning as light workers, will be far more interested in how to excite and engage our own consciousness in work which will be helpful to those who have long known what it is that we do, but have not felt the need for metaphysical study. This would seem to me to mitigate strongly against the whole concept of survival places for a few. I honestly believe that there are many people within this country who are in positions to be responsible for the safety of governmental leaders and people important in one way or another to the world which they and their predecessors have created, in finance, science, research and so forth, who will provide handsomely for the repopulation of the planet in the event of an actual global catastrophe. What we have to give is ourselves, now, in the time of trouble, not ourselves at a later time, when the world will be quite different and those skills which we have been studying in this experience will undoubtedly be quite irrelevant. Perhaps my attitude is too heavily colored by my being a Christian, but it seems to me that we deal, when we speak of life and death on the Earth plane, with "the valley of the shadow of death." I hope to spend my life and my death well, not in terms of how I survive, but in terms of how much of what I had to offer I was able to offer.

It is true that in the second case Susan had the potential of affecting the spiritual journey of others, in that they might well be swayed into putting a great deal of energy into the following of the instructions of her channeling. However, none of us is primarily responsible for other peoples' spiritual evolution; we are responsible for our own. Everything that comes to us is our responsibility in that we can filter and interpret events as we choose, not as we must. Therefore, the primary victim of Susan's difficulties was and is Susan.

If you see anything of yourself in either of these examples, or if you are taking this opportunity to examine your motives for channeling or for wanting to channel and finding that there is a bit of ego involved, don't be hard on yourselves or panic. It is intrinsically human to have motives like this. Inside information, especially if confidential, is always alluring. Finding out that you have some refining to do is a good thing, not a condemnation of what you have done in the past. Through the use of tools such as meditation and contemplation you can begin and enable the process of refining your motives for seeking to be of service by channeling, and, meanwhile, the knowledge that such motives do not serve one well as a channel will help you to recognize times when you have gone a bit astray. In the spiritual evolutionary process in general and in the practice of channeling in particular there is no time at which you cannot turn and begin completely anew. I think that the best of us have to do that every day, if not more often than that. In no way do I wish to suggest that my motives are always pure. Indeed, before I began to write this book, I went through several weeks of indecision and paralysis, asking myself the question, "Who do I think I am, setting myself up as an expert?" Obviously, nobody deserving; like Arjuna in the BHAGAVAD GITA, however, I counseled myself in the end to go ahead and act, but to attempt to keep this action free from the dedication to an outcome.

So each of you has the opportunity at all times to examine your motives and actions, discern any missed steps and turn to a more refined or enlightened consciousness. It is a complete waste of time to be angry at yourself, so if you find yourself to be a little moved by considerations of ego, give a laugh at the human condition, and keep on trying.

Chapter Three
Preparing Yourself To Be A Channel

Channeled information, like any other writing, uses the stuff of languages, sentence construction and words, those chameleon-like entities that take on various meanings and shades depending upon the ways in which they are used. Like any other producer of written material, you, as channels, wish to create the best communication you can. Since a channel has little control over the process once the channeling has begun, it is well to look at some of the elements that go into your preparation as a channel.

A very large consideration is the character of your particular mind. The unique nature of your mind complex is profoundly central to you as a channel because of the nature of the practice of channeling. In channeling you are dealing with personalities whom you cannot see. Invisible entities, or thought-beings, have "reality" only insofar as they are pure in their explication of who they are. In the world of channeling thoughts are indeed things. When one is dealing with friends, family or associates, one has a good deal more to go on than the basic purity of consciousness of the person dealt with, as indicated through the words being used. Even in a telephone call, someone can communicate to you by the tone of voice and the placement of phrasing and hesitations much more than the words themselves can convey. When one is face-to-face, one has body language and other visual signals, as well as the full range of the five senses, to aid one, at least potentially.

But in the world of thought within which a channel is attempting to learn how to become powerful, one has only one's own true nature with which to work in order to be a person powerful enough to control, if necessary, the contacts which one receives. You would not wish any stranger to be able to walk up on your porch, ring your doorbell and talk with you about anything he or she wished, while you had absolutely no control over when the uninvited guest left. Yet in channeling one is very often in the position of receiving an uninvited guest, and it is most persuasively important that you as a channel begin and persevere in the process of knowing just who you are—what the makeup of your mind is, what your basic and pretty unchangeable biases are and what sort of contact you feel you can welcome and share with others as the highest and best contact of which you are capable.

Two intellectual dynamics which profoundly affect your channeling are the rational mind versus the intuitive mind, or wisdom by scientific knowledge versus wisdom by faith. The mind which is comfortable with ratiocination will be looking for that which can be known and that which can be done by man on Earth in any contact it receives. Consequently, the rational-minded channel will tend towards being an instrument which produces information of a highly ethical content. Conversely, if you rely for many things on your intuition rather than your rational processes, your channeling will contain a large percentage of material having to do with ideals. The rational channel may produce very good day-to-day advice but probably not a satisfactory metaphysical system which works without reference to any situation. One who channels from faith without regard to the intellectual mind may well produce large amounts of lovely-sounding, inspirational marshmallow fluff which will help those already faithful, but have no power to inspire the uncommitted seeker. There is the need, in any channel, for balance between these two dynamics.

Look around your living room. Do you find a large number of metaphysical or religious objects about you? The majority of you will answer either "No" or "Very few." The twentieth century is part of an age in which ideals have fallen prey to ethics and the relative has overtaken the absolute. Most of us live in the mundane world not by faith but by a dependence upon scientific achievement. I have no objection to the century, its achievements or its biases. I would have died several times over had it not been for sophisticated technology, for I was a victim of kidney disease in late childhood and twice came close to death. I embrace the television and all the other media, thankfully dine on meals made simple by microwave cookery, not so thankfully receive and dispense telephone calls thanks to Mr. Bell's drop-dead idea, and earned my living, before I became involved in paranormal research, as a librarian, which is in essence an interpreter and conserver of information for people who may find libraries a bit confusing. I realized just how far behind the technological power curve I had gotten several years ago when I was accompanying two young friends to a movie. After the picture, James and Jennifer, then no more than eight and ten, asked to drop by a neighboring video arcade. James settled down with "Tron" and Jennifer, a mature and serious young lady, courteously inquired as to my entertainment before securing her own. Bewildered by the dazzling array of games, I turned toward another "Tron" and said "I think I'll play that."

Jennifer winced slightly and said, "I think that's a little advanced for you." This is from a ten-year-old.

"Well, then, what would you suggest?"

Jennifer considered, her head cocked to one side. She then led me to a Pac-Man game saying, "I would rather have given you a 'Frogger' first, but there isn't one available."

"How hard can this be?" I thought to myself. Then I found out. After playing an entire game without discovering any connection between what my hands were doing and what was happening on the display, I turned again to Jennifer for help. She taught me patiently and I tried again, with only limited success. It would cost me a fortune to learn video skills, unless my family and school both had computers, and I began early. This generation's children often have that set-up.

Much has been written about the increasing pace of technical advancement in the civilized world today, perhaps too much, so I will not belabor the point. Although I am aware that we tend to treat sages of science with the awe formerly reserved for dons of divine lore, and while we certainly reward professionals in the sciences with monetary gains outlandishly exceeding those which can be earned by most parish priests and preachers, I think it is a waste of time to cavil. In a free society we pay for what is most valuable to us and if my priest is not getting as much as my doctor, it is not the fault of his knowledge or value but of my perception of it, and the responsibility lies squarely with me.

It is easy to make the case for our world's being one in which rational thought is enormously more respected than the faculties of intuition. Consequently, when you look at yourself as a potential channel you need to do so with an eye for the need to bring yourself into balance. A good instrument has an attitude in which the rational and intuitive faculties are in cooperative harmony, and the whole of your mind and heart is at the service of the gift of channeling. Were out-of-balance channels all equally helpful this advice would be superfluous although probably helpful in the general sense since we all have both faculties, and it is well to use the whole being in one's thoughts and actions for the most effectively lived life. However, if you are completely rational and accept no intuitive influence, or if you are completely intuitive and accept no rational thought, you will be an off-balance channel, channeling off-balance information, helpful only to those distorted in just the same way as you. The closer to an equitable blend of these faculties that you can come, the more people besides yourself there are who will find your channeled material helpful to them. You see, your mind is just a radio in terms of the telepathic process. Just as a radio must be tuned, so the mind must be tuned to the station that you wish to get. Furthermore, there is a drop-off of stations towards both ends of the band, and a large percentage of desirable contacts are to be found pretty much in the middle, in terms of a balance between intuition and rationality. Balancing your mind is part of the tuning process.

When you have analyzed your own habits of thinking and have decided whether you rely largely on intuition or rational thought, then you may have a good deal more insight than you had before as to what principle you may find which seems to you to be worthy of your fidelity. If you value scientific, objective thinking and empirically proven information, it would be outrageous to expect that you would be able to turn wholeheartedly to a religious system based on faith alone. Conversely, if you find your opinion being that nothing, in the end, is what it seems, and that science is deluding itself if it thinks it has the deeper answers, it would be reasonable to expect that you would have difficulty accepting the universe as a thing which yields best to scientific study. Now although it is widely accepted that religious people live a moral life by virtue of faith in their intuitively perceived source of wisdom, it is not so often clearly seen that those who believe in the world of relative values and empirical data can have faith in themselves and their ability to acquire wisdom and live a morally committed life. However, both paths are viable; passion and commitment of self can ensue from either bias of thought.

To continue the tuning process by examining the character of your own mind, it is well to settle on that principle to which you, just as you are, can be wholly faithful. If it is an orthodox religion to which you are drawn then it is well for you to become an active and practicing religious person. If it is a philosophical system that appeals to your rational mind, then it behooves you to choose that one statement of what is true that you consider to be worthy of your complete fidelity, and practice its dictates and ethics conscientiously and lovingly. Whatever you choose, keep the pressure up to be constantly faithful and regular in your pursuit of and devotion to that which you believe. The more profound and vehement you can make that choice and that decision, the more grounded you will be as a channel, and the more powerful your "magical" personality and, as a result, your telepathic receiver will become. I have said often, in speaking to groups, that when you know what it is you would die for, then you know what it is you wish to live for. All things are acceptable, in an absolute sense, as far as I am concerned. However, not all things are helpful avenues for a channel's mind to run in. For instance, it is a perfectly acceptable philosophical point of view that experience through the senses is everything and that wisdom will come only from excess. The artist's suffering is the understatement of this philosophical system, with wondrous drunken poets like Rimbaud, Dylan Thomas and James Morrison trying always to "break on through to the other side." It is the agony of confrontation carried further and further, to the limit of the mind's ability to express or receive meaning. It is a philosophy that fires the imagination, as well it might, since those who adhere to it destroy themselves in the service of communicating their special wisdom to others. It is not, unfortunately, a very helpful attitude for a channel, for there is no allegiance given to any truth to which one can cling in the face of the enormous influence of excess. It is to be noted that excessive asceticism runs into the same problem. There have been many saints, in religions the world over, who have inspired disciples by their presence, but were far too finely turned to offer themselves as instruments for that which overshadowed them.

Because you are reading this book it is quite likely that you have more faith than discrimination. Most who wish to channel harbor that wish out of a desire to pursue the unseen and so increase the world's store of inspiration and wisdom. If this is your particular orientation I would suggest that you go through a period of intentionally seeking out information concerning how society works. This store of information need not become encyclopedic. However, it would be well to read a book or two on American history, on present-day politics, on the history of science, on space exploration and on the social problems of today. The intuitively felt desire for a peaceful world becomes far more articulate when one learns a bit about the function and nature of wars in history and the dilemma of the arms race. The gut feeling that no one in the world should be hungry gets real teeth when you leave your comfortable dwelling place and walk for hunger while missing a meal or better yet, volunteer to aid the homeless and hungry in finding their way back through the cracks in society's social floor. Get your hands dirty, so to speak, and not only your awareness will be raised, but also your ability to function as a channel. Social naiveté is almost as inexcusable as cynicism.

For a channel, balance is most important. If you are in a situation where your mind is not telling you that there is a distinction between right and wrong you may be in a good environment for your own growth, but you are not in a good environment for a channel. The more you polarize—that is, exercise your rational and intuitive discriminative ability in choosing what *you* think is right—the more powerful will be the antenna which brings in your signal. Do not baffle yourself by asking what is right for all of mankind. Take it as given that you cannot tell another soul on this planet what is right for him. Then realize that you are responsible for your own stance. When you decide what is right, your world view will come into perspective and your discrimination will equal your faith. The great value of the intellect is that it is a marvelous workhorse and to leave it out of the equation is as foolish as the opposite choice. Remember, I am not attempting to judge the thinking process of those who do not channel but only attempting to indicate what makes it more possible to be an effective instrument. For those of you who consider yourselves to be largely creatures of rational bias and highly articulate social awareness, but not primarily competent at grasping the dynamics of worship or beingness' ascendancy over all manifestation, it would be an excellent idea for you to invest in a series of classes or lessons in whatever discipline you feel would be most instructive to you. Some of the world's best thinkers have reached an awareness of the possibility and necessity of a balanced mind and a balanced life by investigating the Roman Catholic or Episcopal faith, which are by far the most rich in magical and mystical illusions which have been rationalized by a series of stupendously gifted writers. Others may find Sufi retreats to yield a more clear understanding of the seemingly holy nature of all experience, when the "doors of perception" have been cleared and purified. Mountain climbing, jumping out of airplanes, and any and all investigations into religious or meditative disciplines offer a varied and helpful tapestry of choices for those of you who wish to balance an overwhelmingly rational consciousness. What I am encouraging in you who think rather than feel the majority of the time is not that you become dedicated to the worship of any unseen God or practice, but that you become aware enough of the consciousness which attends spontaneous worship that you may transfer the seeking of that consciousness to your commitment to that statement of the truth about the creation and the Creator so that you may be a passionate advocate of that in which you believe. Advocacy, or a clear expression of who you truly are, what you believe in most deeply, and that to which you are committed, is the structure or skeleton of your magical personality, and without passion, without bias, your ability to deal effectively with invisible entities is quite small.

When you are satisfied with your intuitive/rational balance of mind and you feel that your power to discriminate is roughly equal to your power to believe, it is time to conclude your conscious analysis. All of the work so far has been done using the intellect. You have subjected both your intuitive and rational minds to the examination of rational thought processes. Now it is time to subject both intuition and rational thought to the catalyst of intuition and faith. The most effective way of immersing yourself, during your waking hours, in the subconscious powers of your mind is to meditate. If you are one of those people who has decided that you are some orthodox religious follower such as a Theosophist or a Christian, you are already going to church and may well have daily religious devotions and prayers. Meditation is recommended in addition to these things. Meditation is silent. The basic idea of meditation is that no rational processes are accepted in the practice. For this reason, those who teach meditation are usually interested in finding ways to still the conscious mind with all of its complex worries and chains of thought.

An immersion in silence is powerful. Even one such experience may be life-changing although that is not the norm. Perhaps the most important feature of your meditative practice should be its dailiness. No matter how well or poorly you feel that you are meditating, it is well to intend to do it the same way each day, not to dwell on any past "bad" meditations or missed ones. Aim for doing it every single day. The length of your silence may vary although it is a good idea to become regular in your habits in order that you might do it at all. If you set yourself too ambitious a schedule of meditation you will surely miss one when you are fatigued, and after the first miss or two, you will be far less enthusiastic about doing it again. You can say to yourself, "Oh well, I have already missed so many, one more day won't hurt." Meditating a modest fifteen or twenty minutes a day will be of inestimable value to you if you are faithful in doing it every day.

The real work of meditation is the relaxing of the structure of the conscious mind so that thought processes do not occur necessarily governed by the rules of mentation. We, as biocomputers, are perceptors and recorders of an astonishing array of anarchic, unstructured sensations—visual, aural and the rest. We have several large programs and subprograms within our computers which ruthlessly organize the data presented, throwing out over ninety-nine percent of it and concentrating on those things which it has tagged as relevant to the programs It is organized to run. Meditation allows new programs to surface, programs designed to assist in decision-making, the only purpose of the computer, and programs designed to feed more data into the base from within the mind itself, its far memory and so forth. However, the conscious programs block out the program assists and the special programs which are offered by the subconscious mind. For the two to work together, these controls must be lifted. Meditation will accomplish this if done faithfully and daily for long enough. It is not often an astonishingly quick process. This explains, by the way, why great trauma creates a heightened rapidity of learning. During traumatic times, the programs of the mind are being urged to change. Computer programs cannot change without dying and being restructured. The computer strives to maintain, and must dump the program instead. This releases an enormous amount of power, because any time the conscious programming is loosened, the program assist from the subconscious mind springs into action, and a very enhanced field of data, and program for organizing data, goes into effect. This is why it is not necessary to achieve a perfect meditation each time. It is an aesthetic joy to worship by offering a perfect service, whether ritualistic or silent, to the Creator—but not biologically necessary. It is only necessary that the intention be strong and that the mind will accept instruction at some level and begin to loosen the logical programming compulsion, thereby automatically completing circuits into the subconscious mind and into the frontal lobes. It is as though heart and mind were at once linked—a very helpful state.

There have been many books written on how to meditate. Although I teach meditation, I do not teach a certain practice. I have known one or two people who were in meditation nearly all of the time and who hoped to hone their consciousnesses to the point where meditation would be a steady state. I have never known one who succeeded. But it is a valid way of meditating, although perhaps the most difficult. I have known people who found it most illuminating to meditate with eyes open, staring at what was in front of the eyes without attempting to force it into making sense. This is not recommended for the Occidental meditator because our entire way of life is active rather than passive. For the product of the western hemisphere, aids such as background music or soothing sounds of some kind such as recordings of wind through trees or even white noise are often very helpful, since it gives the rational mind something to chew on, something to follow and become entrained to while the deep mind does its work unhindered by the noisy chatter of rationality.

Aids internal to the meditator fall mostly in the area of visualization. It may be helpful to picture the breathing of air as a black and white flow in and out of a reservoir, the good clean, energized air being breathed in as a bright white light filling the reservoir of the lungs, becoming dimmed by all this is negative within you, and then all that dimness exhaled into the outer darkness so that you may picture yourself becoming lighter and lighter as you breathe in new energy and get rid of dead energy.

I have spent many an enjoyable meditation watching the inside of my eyelids. Hallucinations have always come easily to me and I am soon off watching an ever-shifting kaleidoscope of colors and shapes.

A morning meditation while the body has not yet taken on the slings and arrows of that particular day's outrageous fortune gives a fine start to a day. Some find it extremely helpful to meditate again in the evening, gazing back over the day before going into meditation, and asking guidance for what could be done better. Any moment may be used for clearing the mind; any five minutes is a potential meditative refreshment.

I'd like to emphasize that your expectation will mold the actual results of your meditation. It is my opinion that in the metaphysical world, intention is everything. What we wish to do may never seem to come to fruition as we intended it and in an everyday sense this is often tragically so. However, regardless of how one's intentions are manifested, if one has the expectation of doing the very best one can, striving one's hardest, believing one's highest, the world of the spirit will record the intention, not the manifestation. I think that one of the things that Jesus' parable of the Sower and the Seed was meant to demonstrate was the nature of intention. The sower had control over the seed, in that he chose good seed. However, he had to sow as he walked, and he could not choose whether he walked over good soil or bad. His intention remained steady. The growth of the seed once it was sown, was governed by the circumstances of the soil onto which it fell. So no matter what the results of the meditations, keep expecting and intending your very best effort. The exercise of your faith, backed up always by the power of your discrimination, will propel you into a more and more powerful position as an instrument.

At the end of each day, take your observations from your daily moments and the consciousness which you can remember from meditation and bring both to bear on the things which have moved you one way or the other, for good or for ill, during your day. If you have hurt someone, it is well to attempt to go through that conversation or action again, with an eye to bringing the balance of compassion to bear on both you and whomever else was involved. Rededicate yourself to the service of others and open yourself to the power of whatever redemption you believe exists, by forgiving any who have harmed you, and by praying to whatever you may call God, for redemption and forgiveness. In this way, you are constantly dying to yourself as a personal being and opening yourself up as a more polarized, more service-oriented impersonal being in which you are not caught on the tenterhooks of your own feelings and ego but are freer and freer to serve that principle of truth that we all seek, in whatever manner, and its reflection in all of those we wish to serve.

The remaining consideration for you who prepare to be a channel is complex enough that it deserves its own chapter. So we are not finished with the subject! However, to finish this chapter I would like to mention one remaining, obvious, but sometimes overlooked, skill which may be cultivated if the skill is not already under your belt. Since you are offering yourself as an instrument in order to be of service to your fellow beings you need to be aware that the notes you play are words, sentences, paragraphs and concepts. If you are not fully comfortable with your own degree of literacy, by all means put yourself to the task of reading. It is relatively "good" books that are usually recommended but one cannot, unless one is very special, live on a steady diet of culturally uplifting material. In order to make your tongue wrap itself around a larger vocabulary and become more able to articulate concepts, it is equally helpful to read any good mystery, pot boiler, science fiction, romance or suspense story—or anything that exercises your vocabulary and your reasoning processes. I am not one of those who looks down upon the lesser genres of literature, for I have been a voracious reader of both "good" and evanescent literature all my life and enjoy both enormously.

I have heard several people object when I say that it is helpful to increase one's ability to articulate concepts and find just the right word by conscious thought. Such people have the notion that the person channeling asymptotically approaches a pure contact, with no contribution by the channel. My opinion is that about one quarter of most good channeling is contributed by the channel, both the channel's words and experiences. This may be an incorrect view; however, the great bulk of channeled information is produced by those in a light trance, or at least those not asleep, and it seems to me that as it is impossible to eliminate the personal factor from channeling, it surely would be considered desirable by both the instrument and the one who offers the channeled material to the instrument for the instrument to have a disciplined and predictable share, obviously in the minority, but not insignificant, in the material. If you are a new channel and one of your objections to channeling is that you fear that you are channeling yourself, attempt to lessen the influence your personal thinking may have on the channeling, but—and again, this is only my opinion—do not try to eliminate it, for you are a valuable part of the channeling process.

In no way do I wish to indicate that you are responsible for what flows through you past a certain point. However, as an instrument you are responsible for the quality with which you are able to transmit what you receive. You will be receiving, most likely, concepts rather than words, and your ability to clothe concepts in examples and telling vocabulary will make the difference between a so-so channeling and an inspiring one.

CHAPTER FOUR
GETTING PEACEFUL

There are certain problems that will predictably distract and metaphysically impoverish one who wishes to become an instrument. To explain why they have such a devastating effect on your work and on you, regardless of context, takes a bit of examination of some of the basic assumptions with which I have learned to work. As with the entire handbook, everything in this chapter is my personal opinion and if anything does not seem to ring true to you, please disregard it without a second thought.

I've come to picture myself as a field of energy, manifesting itself to me subjectively as both my consciousness and my body. Any number of ever-flowing circumstances affect my consciousness, distorting it with moods. The energy field of the body, which many call the electrical body and some term the aura, seems to have centers within which are located the emotional and physical nerve endings that go with each particular kind of energy. When the infinite light of the Creator flows from the universe to us, I believe it enters at the feet and encounters the first energy center at the base of the spine. If that energy center is not blocked by conflicting or abnormal energy patterns, the Creator's light continues to move upward, through all of the energy centers, leaving the body above the crown of the head and flowing back into the creation. The concept is an old one as is the concept of energy centers or "chakras," both terms being part of the Buddhist tenets of faith.

There are seven energy centers within the body in my scheme of things, starting with the energy center located at the joining of the legs. You could see this, for the sake of easy remembering, as the color red, and each of the other energy centers as moving through the colors of the rainbow (red, orange, yellow, green, blue, indigo and violet, with the white being an impersonal eighth color and chakra located above the crown of the head.) The red-ray energy center is the controller for your basic survival mechanisms. A strong red-ray energy center is necessary for any kind of healthful living. It deals with matters of survival and sexuality, and its welfare is important to channels.

The orange-ray energy center is located a bit below the navel. It is the center of personal relationships, the energy center which one uses in sharing experience with another person.

The yellow-ray energy center, often called the solar plexus center, or chakra, is located right where you would fold up if someone hit you in the stomach. Assigned to it are the energies having to do with society and all of society's groups, everything from armies to church congregations to teams that you may watch or be a part of. These first three centers constitute the all-important basic personal triad of energies which tend to keep us from getting peaceful.

The green-ray energy center, also called the heart chakra, is the seat of unconditional love. It is not to be confused with romantic love which often has energies having more to do with the desire to possess another person, and, therefore, imposing conditions on a relationship, which is an orange-ray energy, or with "you owe me" feelings about your mate which is an energy connected with our society's laws of marriage, and is a yellow-ray energy. Green-ray love imposes no conditions and the compassion that it generates is unconditional. Perhaps you remember times when you have sung the old Christmas carol, "The Twelve days of Christmas." One was never really sure of most of the other gifts that the song's hapless swain was giving his true love, but one was always sure of the "'five gold rings." The heart chakra is much like that; central, as love must be to our experience. Unconditional acceptance is usually something that feels tremendously good to us and we react to its presence by flowering and growing. It is not easy to awaken that energy within ourselves. Without embarking on that process I encouraged in the last chapter, that of accepting the fact that progress in spiritual evolution involves deciding what manner of person we are, choosing our path, and then learning more and more about how to be faithful to the path and how to express love to others as the fruit of what we are learning on that path, it is almost impossible to accomplish. Meditation is a tremendous help, because the nature of consciousness, left in total balance, is peaceful, serene and joyful. We seldom experience this because we are filling our minds up almost all of the time with daily business, which is no bad thing were we able to retain, in the midst of mundane activity, the consciousness of love. We seldom do that, however, and so we are constantly distracting ourselves and thereby removing our attention from our native disposition, which is a happy one.

Even when we are alone, we distract ourselves with thoughts of what could have been or what should have been, scolding, praising and judging ourselves and others, sometimes over and over, instead of enjoying the opportunity for solitude. Sometimes, too, our minds are taken up completely with planning for the future, rehearsing conversations that we have not yet had and may never have, calculating financial progress for the next five years, wondering how to put aside the money for our child's college education, or any number of other perfectly respectable concerns.

Whatever our reason for not perceiving the joy of the moment, it is so that we seldom do perceive it, and that it is always there, close at hand, ready to be perceived. We must look for it, however, and to do that we must first have the firm impression that we are looking for something that exists. Consequently, without analysis and meditation to feed our wills, it is often very difficult to get started on activating the green-ray energy center, or, to put it another way, on opening up the heart chakra. It is this chakra which must be functioning well in order for the service of channeling to run smoothly in your life. Centers higher than that can be very helpful if they are also activated, but it is not necessary for them to be activated for you to be a productive (and healthy) channel.

The blue-ray energy center, located at the throat, has to do with communication that is freely given with no expectation of return.

The indigo-ray energy center or brow chakra is located at the "third eye" location and has to do with metaphysical work in general and our ability to manifest our true inner beingness, and the crown chakra or violet-ray center is basically a summing of all the preceding energies, the last expression of personhood before the Creator's energy dissolves again into the uncolored white light that is the first manifestation of the Creator known to us.

Although it would seem centrally important to open the heart chakra, if you wish to channel, it has seemed to me that more emphasis also needs to be placed upon removal of blockages in the first three energies, red, orange and yellow. The reason for this is that it is perfectly possible to work hard in opening up your compassionate energies, and do a very good job at it, but run into serious problems because you have left undone work which first should have been completed in the lower energy centers. Channeling is an activity recommended for those who are stable and who have come to the conclusion that they wish to be of service to the Creator and to humankind. A person who is merely curious, but who, unknown to himself, may possess a highly sensitive psychic nature, may be propelled into opening the green-ray energy center because of all the experiences that begin happening to him while he is satisfying his curiosity. It can happen very quickly. As always, the key seems to me to be balance. One puts one's foot at the first place, gets a good balance, and then moves on. By jumping from lessons still not learned in the first three centers to opening the fourth center with the first three still unbalanced, the way is opened for any problems that you do have of a personal nature to be greatly distorted and intensified simply because you are a channel, involved in offering inspiration and light to others, and so attracting the attention of the principle which is antithetical to light, the principle of darkness. As a channel, you're transmitting on one level, yet as an individual you vibrate at a lower level. This is inevitable, yet the distance between the two levels needs to be as little as possible. For, metaphysically speaking, you are responsible for living at the highest level of which you've been made aware. If you are a new channel and begin thinking that you have outgrown your mate, that you must have someone who believes in you, that you "have your rights," and so forth, you may be heading down dangerous streets.

OK, you say that you don't want your marriage to break up, you don't think, but you are having trouble with it or with something else having to do with personal energy. What do you do about it? You know I would be foolish were I to think that I could put down on paper something that would be helpful to everyone. For writing that inspirational, you had better go to records of channeled lives such as Jesus the Christ, and see what He said! However, I can give a few opinionated pointers and hope that they may be of some help to some of you.

Dealing with sex did not used to be a great problem at least in terms of what men and women were supposed to do with their sexuality. It was understood that men could choose to be either promiscuous, monogamous or celibate. Conventions for each of these three lives were known and understood. Women had one less choice, unless the choice was to become a prostitute; women married and, if fertile, bore children, or they did not marry and lived a celibate existence, perhaps functioning as mother's helper for a sister or another female relative, living perhaps alone but certainly not promiscuously. This century has been one of fairly rapid social revolutions, beginning with the free love propounded in the 1920s, snapping back into a demi-prudery during the Depression and war years, and gradually opening up into the increasingly measured "free love" and serial relationships of the sixties. By now, men and women seem to have achieved a large measure of sexual equality, with both men and women being far more interested perhaps than they ever have been in the quality of relationships. A woman's sexual morality is measured these days not so much by the number of her partners as by the quality of relationships that she has developed with those who are or have been her lovers. Consequently, it seems to me that people as a whole are doing less blocking of the red-ray energy than they were used to, letting most energy move directly into orange-ray activity.

However, there is still in all of us that vulnerable part that gazes somewhat askance at the power of the red-ray drive. When I was close to thirty, for instance, I found myself, for a period of two or three years, thinking constantly about having a child. My health history was such that it was out of the question for me to conceive, and yet I wanted a baby with all of my heart and couldn't get it off of my mind. It was not until I was about thirty-two that the last irrational and potentially self-destructive attack came and went and I was delivered over to the comfortable, though sad, feeling that it really was too late to set about having a child in my condition of health. That is the power of red-ray instinct.

We need to take any feeling of embarrassment that we have about that very vital energy and get rid of it, replacing it with good feelings towards the energy that keeps us alive. The survival instincts to breathe, to reproduce, to eat and so forth have bailed us out of many a situation by quickening our reflexes and plunging our body into a rapid dispersal of blood and oxygen when we need them the most. The sexual energy as such needs to be seen and appreciated as part of what keeps us alive. The romantic preoccupation with the sexual experience of orgasm as a kind of death has so influenced our culture that it makes us feel negatively about the very energy that made it possible to be living now—what in the world would we have done if everyone in the world had decided that sex was not an acceptable moral expression of our natures!

In running through your unconscious biases about sex, there are certain key points to check. One: have you chosen to see sex as a positive thing? Do you ever say, "I wish I were a man" if you are a woman or "I wish I were a woman" if you are a man? If you have any kind of negative feeling about sexuality, work on your perceptions until you have found a way to embrace the idea of sex. This is not to say that it is necessary for your spiritual growth to be sexually active. The records of history rather indicate that this is not a relevant consideration and some doughty souls would indeed say that sexuality was just one more distraction. Note that people who say that sex is a distraction from the spiritual life are giving a bad opinion about sex. Whether or not you have any sexual activity going or planned, try to wrap your mind around the idea that sex is a distraction from the spiritual life only for those who have not yet gotten their sexual energy center clear and unblocked. If the sexual energy is clear it neither helps nor harms but is its own expression, its own energy, and the light that gives energy to every pattern that we have enlivens and blesses that kind of energy and then moves onward.

This next bit is of information is probably not intended for those of you who are carefree, dating lots, or a little, or not at all, but quite un-mated at the present, for the personal miseries of jealousy and possessiveness afflict those of us in relationships already, for the most part. Nor is it meant for any who are in happy agreement with the limitations and responsibilities their personal relationships require. But for most of us, life does not consist of relationships which are perfectly satisfactory, and you may find yourself in the paragraphs below.

Have you ever said, "Not tonight, honey. I have a headache," when you really mean, "I'm too upset with you to be able to make love?" If you have, you are certainly not alone. However, you are using sex as a bargaining chip. This is not using sex as a clear energy. A clearer expression would be to say what you mean, that you are upset and so cannot share love. Then you have opened the way for honest, two-way communication. Once the talking is done, you may find your sexual energy flowing well once more. This, by the way, is why making up can be such fun, for communication opens the heart chakra, and it feels so good for energy to be moving freely again. Whatever you are gaining by sexual bargaining, you are losing the ability to funnel light through to the heart center, and so are setting yourself up for very unsettling experiences in the context of your spiritual life and especially your channeling. If you cannot deal with the thought of making love to your mate because there is no love in this moment for you with him or her, then you need to say that, and then move the emphasis from sex to where the trouble really lies. Usually in a situation where you have feigned a headache, the real problem is either that your mate is clinging to you, wanting you to possess him or her, or you feel that your mate is ignoring you and attempting to put separation between him or her and you. Either distortion causes the same effect—alienation from your mate and a tendency to use sex to express your hurt feelings. There is also the tendency of some people to use sex as a reward. This is used more by women than by men, although both sexes have their proponents of this tactic. This also is an unclear use of sexual energy. Try to ally sex in your physical experience with love so that you either discover how you love the unlovable mate, and give yourself in that spirit, in the interests of prolonging the relationship until you have found a way to fall in love again, or explain carefully that you need to be celibate until you have learned to love again. Sex is not, in my opinion, in itself an excuse for the severance of a bad relationship. It is something that is a symptom of unclear energies between two people, because all sex is good sex to the red-ray chakra. Thus, if you are having difficulty with sex and it is not organic, that difficulty is likely a mismatch of orange-ray energies.

Turning again and again to the ideal of unconditional love in your sexual life is highly recommended, for if you offer yourself in that energy, you are vibrating a clear red and orange ray, and the energy then is moving upwards on schedule, heading for the all-important green-ray heart chakra. This is your goal. You very much want to make the path of light free from obstruction so that in full force it may reach the heart chakra and activate it fully. Your greatest ally in achieving green-ray activation is your enthusiasm and will to seek clear and unconditional love. The energy of the Creator is pulled upwards along the spine by the seeker's desire for ever-purer realizations of love and wisdom. It is in the deep intention of the meditator and in conscious intention to a lesser degree that the will to seek is honed.

Let me take a moment to square off and talk about a very central problem for so many people who have started off on the path of spiritual seeking. Whether it is orthodox or heterodox, this seeking will change you. If you are in a relationship, but you cannot coax your friend, lover, mate or spouse to join you on this path, you will be walking a new path all by yourself in no time at all. Meditate for two months, and you will find yourself a person with a different mind, a different point of view. This does not do anything good for your relationship, for you will perceive that you have "grown apart," that your mate does not any longer understand you and may not even approve of what you are doing. The further and faster that you go, the more obvious this difference becomes. Far too many marriages break up because of the catalyst encountered on the spiritual path. Many bitter words have been said by those who are attempting to become more compassionate. Many words of judgment have been cast at a perplexed and uncomprehending mate who is struggling to understand your new beginnings with his or her old ideas. The spiritual path seems so fresh, new and wonderful—which it is—that any sacrifice seems little enough to make in order to become more securely "on the path." And so many a relationship ends, unfinished, forever a source of frustration to both parties, who wonder despite words to others whether the right decision was really made.

If you are in this position, you are no doubt uncomfortable, and I do not want to minimize the validity of that discomfort. However, in my very human opinion now is a good time to keep your head and try to see things from the largest perspective available to you. There may be a lot riding on this decision, in terms of your responsibilities and commitments.

In the first place, if you are married you made a contract. Look at it for the moment as a business contract. You agreed to sell goods and services to a corporation, the marriage, in exchange for nothing whatsoever, except love. There is nothing in a marriage contract about what a person will get from the relationship but rather two people's promises of what they will give to the relationship. At the time of the wedding, presumably, both parties to the contract feel that they will be recompensed by society and by each other, by the fruits of marriage, such as a house and children, if indeed they thought about it at all. However, the actual contract, unless you have made a marriage agreement, is unequivocally a contract of giving with no expectation of return. What else does "for better or for worse, for richer or for poorer, in sickness and in health and till death do us part" mean? There are no guarantees. The first casualty of a broken marriage is your word. As I have described in the previous chapter, the deciding of what you think is right, and then being faithful to it, is very important in your preparation of character for the service of channeling. Does breaking your word strike you as something that is "right"? If it is not "right," why are you doing it? If you are not being abused either physically or emotionally, but are merely finding life uncomfortable because you can no longer talk to your mate, I urge you strongly to consider carefully whether or not you wish to break your word. I have seen people who stayed together for a long time, and actually began making inroads in communicating with each other again. I have also seen seemingly hopeless relationships in which both parties stayed with the marriage because it was the "right" thing to do. It is true that the two couples that I have in mind are both unhappy in their personal relationships. However, it is also true that each of the two has, because they have made peace with the primary relationship, developed tremendously strong and helpful activities on other levels, and has become a much more powerful person, a person that she probably would not have become had she turned away from what she felt would be the "right" thing to do.

It is a high price to pay for believing in your ideals. But in the long run, the majority of these things do in the end work out in a very comfortable manner. Perhaps the mate who is trying to hold you back because he is afraid of what you are doing decides that it is not worth it and leaves. The decision has been made for you, and you may go in peace. Perhaps the mate comes to understand you, or at least feels unthreatened by you, learning to see your activities as crazy, maybe, but harmless. If you can live with being misunderstood, which is not as difficult as it sounds, your problems are at an end, and you can go back to loving your mate as you loved that person in the beginning, without stint. At any rate, for the sake of the opening of the pipe which you are to become in order to be a channel for those concepts of heart and mind which may inspire others, it is very well to choose to relate to people as if they did not threaten you but as if you wished only to be of service to them. Far from being less important the more intimate the relationship, the principle becomes more important the more intimate the relationship is. How important it is to choose to see someone intimately important to you as positive, to see the relationship as positive! If you experience any difficulty or trouble in the relationship it is well to apprehend that trouble as an opportunity for learning. Judgment does not have any part in a clear expression of unconditional love, although it's always a good idea to use your usual powers of discrimination in evaluating hurtful words that may be said to you in anger. If they are not true, discount them, but try not to hold a grudge. Nothing makes energy stop dead faster than that kind of negative emotion. Try to notice the good times that you may have even in a bad relationship. It is very easy to underestimate how valuable your mate's presence is to you if that person is getting on your nerves. Let your mate go away, and you have a lot of opportunity to re-evaluate your judgment, but a diminished opportunity to save the situation that you have created by allowing separation to occur.

Is this your situation: you have been a good mate, have given your all to the relationship, have been as good a parent as you could be and are now working to become more spiritually aware, but your mate has seemingly lost interest in you and is chasing after others? You are ready to chuck him/her out on his/her ear because he/she is rejecting you and being unfaithful. Now your mate is exhibiting symptoms of having orange-ray blockage—a fear of being possessed by you, and a desire to be possessed by or to possess another.

OK. That is your mate's problem, not yours unless you take it personally. It very likely has nothing to do with you. Do you want to end the relationship because your mate is in emotional trouble? Maybe you can't take it, and then I say, "fine," but do not try to learn to channel during this period of your life. Things are not settled enough for you right now. In order for your energy to be clear in this situation, you need to settle down, take a deep breath, and actively, prayerfully love your mate. He/she needs you right now. It is time for your marriage contract to be reviewed. Note that there is no small print. This goes for the mates of those who are drunk, insane, homosexual, drugged or otherwise difficult to live with. In order to preserve your own sobriety and sanity, you may have to effect a physical separation. Try not to effect an emotional one as well. Relationships are your life sustenance, in that they give in your you the most intense and satisfying catalyst of any force within your daily life. Because the universe is kind, you are allowed to learn through hardship how to become unattached to hardship—how to embrace the opportunities for learning more about love that are implicit in every bit of difficulty that the relationship is causing you.

As you attempt to clear up this orange-ray energy, also attempt to keep a vision of yourself as powerful in your mind's eye. A powerful person can afford to give freedom to a mate or a friend, even if that freedom leads the other person to do something that you do not like. If you are powerful enough, nothing will make as much difference to you as your own opinion and your own perception. A powerful person can always choose to go the extra mile—exhaustion is unknown to you if you are strong enough. And if you are strong you can choose to honor commitments even if that choice seems a Quixotic gesture. If another wishes to end the relationship, while it is impossible to generalize, it seems to me that the other person's wish is paramount, and the rule of free will is higher than any other consideration. This is my own idea—I put free will at the top of the list of ethical considerations. If you think differently, please do that!

Game-playing in general is a muddying energy, and at whatever energy level you are playing games you will block the flow of energy through that center. It is difficult to play red-ray games, although people who starve themselves to the point of anorexia nervosa are certainly managing it. It is very easy to play orange-ray games, though the anger and other negative emotions this causes result in much illness. And in dealing with society, the frequent user of yellow-ray energy, it is easy to play games. By the time you begin consciously working on your orange-ray center, you have undoubtedly done a good deal of preliminary unconscious work already. None of us escapes being blocked in orange-ray in one way or another, and we make mistakes in judgment time and time again, blocking ourselves until we perceive the problem, communicate about it and clear it up. If we attempt to work on societal games before we have eliminated personal games, we will find ourselves working on games within games. The passions

41

people feel for groups are a kind of extension of the ways that people feel about each other. If you are using people to get ahead in your job, for instance, you are expressing your opinion about a societal question: how does one get ahead in the world? However, if you had unblocked your relationships so that you did not allow yourself to attempt to use other people, you would not have been tempted to use that societal game to block the yellow-ray center.

It is remarkably easy to play games without recognizing them, so any care which can be taken in removing games that you already know about from your palette of thoughts and actions is a good thing. To be remembered in every circumstance is the basic *credo* of one who wishes to be working on channeling: keep the heart chakra as open as possible, full of compassion and undemanding, unconditional love. The desire to be of service to other people is what will tune your receiver and empower it, so it is well to treat this basic frame of mind as your attitudinal goal. Of course the true goal always is to express yourself in your experiences as you really are, not to be insincere for the sake of appearance.

So, what if you have real disagreements with friends or co-workers and find it almost impossible to achieve green-ray compassion with regard to them? Whoever the difficult person is, he is a mirror of you. Sometimes it helps to step back and take a good look at what is bothering you about someone else. Quite often one can see in one's self at least a shadow of the exact characteristic that you have found irritating in someone else. This realization not only makes it possible for you to go about the process of forgiving the person who has functioned as a mirror for you, it also offers you a new opportunity for contrition, self-forgiveness, amendment of life, learning and growth, as you hear criticism that you have made of the mirror of yourself, apply it to yourself and take in the lessons that you have given yourself.

There will be, at least in many cases, an extremely small remainder of persons whose critical faults bear little or no resemblance to any characteristic of yours whatsoever. There are some people who are seemingly unfortunate, who have almost an instinct for being undesirable persons. Usually, these people have serious mental or emotional problems. Realizing this pulls the sting, at least for me, and makes the acid quality of the relationship leach away, so that my heart's sweet again, for why would I wish to heap further problems upon the head of one who is already greatly troubled? It is likely that whatever unfortunate person of this kind you know would not prefer to be pitied; most would rather arouse anger than truth. But for you, if not for your negatively emoting friend, pity is by far the better emotion, as compassion is a far more gentle service to offer another than anger. If you are using this reasoning for more than one or two people in your life, you need to polish your glasses.

There is one characteristic you will need to watch as you continue learning and growing as a seeker and as an instrument: beware of becoming a fanatic. You will have more and more to share with people. You will be full of one enthusiasm and then another as your mind takes in all that it can of the spiritual literature available to us now, that body of books and other media being the largest it has ever been in our written history, due to the preserving of older books in libraries, and the constant deluge of new offerings as time moves on. The accumulation will leave you in many different moods at different times.

At more than one point in your experience you will feel that you have the answer. Live with that, but try not to evangelize. This practice is one more means of the imposition of your will upon another, and what this whole chapter has been talking about is the supremacy of that most primitive of qualities, free will. It is of utmost importance that both other people and you shall have freedom of choice at all times. You cannot make anyone but yourself choose, nor can you tell people what their choices are. Each person is the center of his or her own creation. Although all choices are fundamentally between separation and unity, darkness and light, in one way or another, each person's perception of the choices and the times of necessity for choice, will be different.

If a person comes to you and says, "I'm fascinated by what you are talking about. Let's talk about it." then you are being given free rein to engage in conversation of whatever length. Here you may witness to your own search and your own findings. But in the arena of everyday life, those who buttonhole you, whether on the street, at work, in your home or at church are not likely to be appreciated. It seems everyone is aware of the fundamentalist Christian groups who solicit contributions and interest door-to-door. Most are polite in telling their stories, but the common experience is that the visits are not welcome, at best. Perhaps many have also had the experience of relatives or friends who attempt to convert you to whatever religion they are purveying. The more usual reaction is a further emotional separation away from whatever bias your friend has attempted to force upon you. Especially in the free world, we are not accustomed to being told what to think, even by friends. And while we are susceptible to hints, advertising, teasing and other disreputable encroachments on free will, we usually have the sense to resent others' attempts to change us when we are not ready for it, and not asking for it.

Please know that in no way do I wish to suggest that you who cannot live any more with a husband or wife should force yourself to do so because of what I say, or that indeed you should do anything that I suggest. I am trying to expose, for what they are, the factors in sex, love, marriage, relationships with people and relationships with society that keep a person who wishes to be a channel from the relatively stable practice of that service. If you are working with difficult relationships, and your life is pretty torn up right now, by all means do what you must, or do nothing if you do not know what to do yet, and accept living in confusion for a while. But it would be recommended by me that you avoid the practice of channeling during this difficult period in your life. I say this especially strongly where marriage is concerned. It seems that for the most part people who live together without having gone through the marriage ceremony have a fairly realistic idea of the supremacy of the rights of the other person. This is not always true, but there is a tendency for it to be so. The married relationship, on the other hand, largely because of the pressures of many centuries of social distortion of the ideal marriage, is likely to be one in which unity has been broken up into two separate entities, the party of the first part and the party of the second! Husband and wife treat each other to some extent as adversaries rather than yoke-fellows, and instead of thinking about how to please and serve the other, number all the grievances which the other has committed against the self. As the relationship grows more stale the two mates may not even be communicating any more, although both feel that they have tried their utmost. Perhaps sexual promiscuity is an excess troubling you or your mate; perhaps impotence or frigidity has characterized you or your mate's experience but not your own. Perhaps the fights about money have become too painful. Perhaps pride has been damaged too often. And frequently, the children that you have produced together are a most confusing responsibility, having become separate from rather than a part of the original love you and your mate had for each other. All these considerations are terribly stormy, and in any of them you will be experiencing negative emotions.

Please note that I didn't say evil or bad emotions. There is an important difference. A negative emotion is bad for your channeling because it blocks energy from moving through to the heart chakra. A person in the grips of negative emotion by definition does not have a totally open heart center.

Unconditional love and negative emotion are as much opposite as the negative pole and the positive pole in the battery of your car. If you want your battery to work, so that your car can start and do its work, you must have a negative and a positive charge. If you want to do work in consciousness you must have chosen whether you are going to be working on raising the negative charge or the positive charge. You know that the life led without conscious thought is pretty much a zero: one fairly positive thing done on impulse; one slightly negative thing done carelessly; another negative thing done by omission; another positive thing done because of helpful circumstance, the sum total being no polarization. Channeling while angry will put you into a very untuned situation. Your basic state of mind is positive, but your mind tuning's less positive, because of the negative emotion. Therefore, you are far more liable to embrace distortions of more positive thoughts in less positive clothing. In other words, you will be channeling the equivalent of a nonpolarized life—a mixed message. A good example of a mixed message is the Ten Commandments in the Old Testament. Moses was dealing with a very demanding populace who kept asking him for more and more specific information. He had a good contact, but all this specific information was very draining. So when his people asked for rules of life he received, not the positive "do this and do that and your life will be blessed," but instead "do not do this and do not do that, and you shall not be unclean." Negatives are built into this basically very positive set of suggestions, which certainly are inarguably just.

Further relatively untuned communications can lay you open for many difficulties simply because you as a channel are not protecting yourself by living as you believe. Perhaps you've had the experience of a parent saying "Don't do as I do; do as I say." I do not recall that argument ever making any sense to me. I railed bitterly against it, in fact, and was much disillusioned when I saw that good advice was not followed by good behavior on my parents' part. In your own life, when you decide that something is true, and then you do not act on it, you are nullifying that truth within yourself. You are taking the power of the knowledge from yourself and from your consciousness. Your consciousness, your violet-ray summing up of instantaneous self, is your ever-present gift to the Creator. When you rob your consciousness you are robbing the first fruit of your incarnation. When you are in that situation, and come to realize it, it is time not to think badly of yourself, but to attempt to smooth out the difficulty and pain that you are feeling until your life is once again your God-given creation and not something that happens to you. Only when your life is once again largely a product of your conscious thinking, should you go after servanthood as a vocal channel. This is just to cut down on the odds of your running into real difficulty in your work and in your life. So get peaceful insofar as it is possible for you. Even if situations are difficult, if you can find peace and serenity within yourself as you look at these situations, you are in good shape. And so, onward to channeling itself.

CHAPTER FIVE
CHANNELING

I said earlier that learning to be an instrument is easy because people are natural instruments, always channeling something. It's true, as I have learned through the years from teaching a few people how to do it.

Though I do not teach any particular school of channeling, in working with students I do try to get across two concepts, each one of which has a passive and an active phase. The first concept is that of tuning. We have talked about the mind as a radio receiver picking up intelligent, invisible signals and relaying them using our physical equipment. Using this analogy it should be obvious that tuning is all-important. There is intuitive tuning and there is discriminative tuning. First, one must tune the passive, intuitive mind. This is the mind in relation to itself. Meditation is intended as the chief tool for perfecting this process. In meditation you are relaxing and releasing the self from its conscious boundaries. But you are doing work of active intuition also, generating a receptive, active particular invitatory vibration, turning actively towards the source of the signal which you will receive and declaring yourself ready to receive fresh thoughts into your waiting conscious mind. In no way does a receptive attitude connote anxiety or anticipation. You must be meditative, relaxed and accepting of whatever may come. Too much concern and one can easily channel a high percentage of one's own barely unconscious material, delivering not a majority of cosmic thoughts but a mishmash of your own half-digested perceptions. Without the overconcern, even if you are channeling some aspect of your own being, you will be channeling a much clearer version of this same material.

When you feel that you have gotten a contact, your discriminating mind comes into action both towards yourself and towards the source of the contact. Using passive discrimination, you continue focusing, tuning first with the big knob, then with smaller and smaller verniers making finer and finer adjustments, attempting to lift your consciousness to the very highest vibration you can. Only you know when that moment has come. Only you know what you can hold as a steady state. As you are adjusting, you might try singing, chanting or praying. I use a selection from my store of songs and chants, plus music on tape, for preliminary tuning, and then use prayer for the finer adjustments. My favorite is The Lord's Prayer, since it is without doctrine or dogma, and can be prayed equally by Muslim, Jew, Christian, Buddhist and honest skeptic, as long as the skeptic will accept the hypothesis that there is a Creator. For the very fine tuning I prefer the prayer of St. Francis of Assisi. I have known several channels who favored the Great Invocation, and there are many other acceptable and beautiful prayers, including the ones that you make up on the spot, the latter being perhaps the best, as they are the expression of your heart at that exact moment.

You are also, once you receive a contact, in need of your actively discriminative faculties in challenging the source that you have contacted. In order to challenge any invisible entity, you must be able to state, in a sincere and unequivocal way, who you are, what you believe in, what you love and for what you would die. This is why the beginning of the process of becoming a channel is figuring out how your nature and mind "tick." You cannot expect to challenge in the name of Christ if you are of a nature that does not find faith a comfortable emotion. You are not going to be able to challenge in the name of truth if you believe there is no truth, and that man can know nothing. Let us say that you are one who believes—as the majority of new age channels seem to do—in the Christ, not as Jesus the man, but as a consciousness which Jesus attained during his incarnation, but which is also attainable by any being who can keep his mind, soul, heart and strength fixed upon the Creator. You wish, then, to challenge in the name of Christ-*consciousness*. You feel, or you guess, that this is something that you can believe in. In this very complex society we are not used to saying things in a way which implies no relativity. We are used to situational ethics, wrong things being "right" under certain circumstances, and people leaving our religious beliefs pretty much alone in the interest of getting along with each other. It may be difficult for you to say unequivocally that you would die before you would deny the supremacy of the force of Christ-consciousness in your life. It is possible for you to doubt the ideal because of the age in which we live. This is not an age of faith, unless it is faith in empirically derived knowledge. We know that all technology is going to be improved upon, and so even the newest gadgets are looked upon with a mixture of awe and the cynical thought that if we wait just a little longer the technology will improve and the price of the gadgets will go down. It is difficult to put our minds back into the world of unshakable ideals and eternal truths. And yet, if channeling has a real place in expanding our knowledge of the way things are, then it has that because it speaks of unchangeable truths, helping us to perceive them better, more simply and more directly.

So if you have trouble saying "I challenge you in the name of (fill in the blank)," stop and repeat the process recommended in Chapter Three, until you are not only comfortable, but in the position of an advocate of whatever unchangeable truth you have decided is that which is, to you, dearer than life itself. That for which you would die is surely that for which you can live, and the spirit world understands that kind of absolute fidelity. When you wish to become a channel you are wishing to communicate with what has often been called the spirit world. In fact, in libraries using the Dewey/Sears system most channeled material is classified under the heading "Spirit Communications," including the work that I have done, which is in the area of alleged extraterrestrial channelings.

Whatever the nature of spirits you wish to contact or have contacted, they have in common the characteristic of being without self-doubt. I have yet to hear or read a spirit communication from any source in which the spirits were agonizing over who they were or what they believed. It is just that kind of authority for which you are looking in a good contact. It is that kind of authority you need to have as you tune in order that you may challenge the source of your contact when you get it, to ensure that the point of view that you will be channeling matches your greatest and highest desire.

The end result of all of your tuning is crystallized in the moment at which you do receive a contact. In the world of un-things opinions and thoughts are everything. There is no objective referent to pave the way to respectability. In the world of metaphysical thoughts and ideas, the strength with which you embrace your point of view is alone effective. When you have tuned correctly, so that each prayer and thought with which you tune is a meaningful and substantial statement of your belief system, then your challenging should be very easy, because you will have attracted an entity which is capable of communicating about that which you embrace. Presumably an advocate of the same committed, biased interest as you will be easily able to answer your challenge, whether it be in the name of Christ, Christ-consciousness, Truth, the White Light or whatever else you feel is for you the essence of what you believe.

I believe that these last few thoughts are among the most essential that I have to offer. The tuning and challenging process is at the heart of responsible channeling.

I have experienced, not once but many times, spontaneous channeling from new group members who have only come to their first meeting, but are very sensitive to the contacts of those who wish to channel through us. There are people who are such naturally proficient channels that the concept of teaching them is basically laughable, except insofar as one may tidy up a rough diamond by appropriate faceting and polishing. Never have I met a person who could honestly say that channeling would be impossible, after having tried to learn for a significant period of time, two weeks intensively, or once a week for two months, say. There are many who discover that they are very uncomfortable with channeling. I have taught two disc jockeys, for instance, how to channel. One was a happy-go-lucky man, rather irresponsible, although charming and gentle as a lamb. He channeled immediately and with great facility, although I could never teach him any discipline and his channelings became repetitive enough that soon he lost interest in the whole process. He became bored with the new game, because he was not doing enough tuning to move out of his own perceptions into the carefully tuned openness necessary for impersonally transmitted information of interest to him. The other student, although in precisely the same job—morning man on a highly competitive rock and roll station— took his work in a different light. Both men were paid good salaries to be unpredictable and outrageous. However, the second student left none of his outrageousness to chance, doing hours of research and a good deal of pre-production before each show, tying it into the morning's headlines and the latest happenings of the town. Faced with the responsibility of channeling, the sober-minded DJ found himself unwilling to abandon his powers of discrimination long enough to allow another's voice to put concepts in his mind.

But the ease of that process is such that anyone who can let go of his powers of discrimination even a little bit can learn to channel. This isn't to say that everyone is going to be an equally excellent channel. Just about everyone can be taught to play chopsticks. However, the practice sessions are many and the hours are unforgiving betwixt that first rush of chopsticks happiness and a recital at Carnegie Hall. It is not easy to do concertizing or channeling well. The one who ends up doing fairly well is often the one who numbers perseverance and persistence as character traits along with sensitivity and an interest in metaphysics. Sheer practice is a tremendous teacher and the twentieth year of channeling is as informative as the first. The mental and emotional effort required to be an instrument does not slack off with time, but, if anything, becomes greater as experience accumulates. The reason for this is repetition.

Almost anything is fun the first time. I do not have to be interested, particularly, in a given subject in order thoroughly to enjoy listening to someone speak about it. I have a healthy curiosity and like learning about almost anything. However, the idea of doing something the hundredth or thousandth time that I was marginally interested in at the outset is crushing! And even though I enjoy being an instrument, there is a certain amount of energy involved in opening one's physical and perceptual doors, freeing up the necessary time, and readying one's self to be host for yet another weekly meditation meeting—our group has been meeting since 1962, and I have been holding weekly meetings since 1974. My dedication needs to be greater now than it needed to be years ago. It is hard for me to imagine someone so very sociable by nature that, after twenty years, the mechanical aspects of holding a meditation will be the same.

It might be helpful to note that not everyone can channel right away. However, the way the creation is made seems to encourage persistence, since, when you begin to want something, that active wanting generates a kind of magnetic field which keeps bringing that which you want closer to you. What happens to many people is that although they are not progressing rapidly in learning to channel, subjectively interesting things will begin to happen that suggest that something is taking place which is noteworthy. These subjectively interesting things will not constitute proof to any other person except for yourself. There will be some sort of private language between the interesting events and the way your mind is working which will ring a bell for you, letting you know that you are in the process of coming close to what it is you seek.

There have been many examples of this in my own experience, but perhaps the most enjoyable account was that of a young man, Len, who was learning to channel in 1980. He came in complaining of the bitter cold winter weather, explaining that his ex-wife had borrowed his good down coat and not yet given it back. We sat down and began our work. He was taking intensive lessons, learning to channel. During the course of the session I channeled some information for him which seemed highly meaningful to him, having to do with the transformation of caterpillar into butterfly. He explained to me after the session that butterflies had always had a special significance to him. As I nodded my understanding, I saw, crawling towards his foot, a large light-brown woolly worm. It was a couple of months late for seeing these little harbingers of Jack Frost, and so I was surprised to see it at all, much less twenty feet into the house, crawling industriously towards one of the couches in our thirty-four-foot living room. The student sighted along the caterpillar, which had struck both of us with its continuation of the butterfly theme, and saw his winter coat, in a little roll bundled up by the door.

Of course none of this can be proven. One or the other of us could have introduced a butterfly into the channeling, followed it with a nice caterpillar appearance, and by the same token either one of us could have received the coat at some earlier time and merely placed it there for the other to see. That none of these things occurred is only of subjective interest, and that not even to me, but only to the student.

When this sort of coincidence begins happening for you, even if you have not yet learned to channel, you will be cheered on your way, I trust, by the synchronicities of ceaseless spiritual coincidence. You will find that the more you let go in general, attempting to give up your life in impersonal service to all, feeling that there is a greater love than you can generate within yourself, and opening yourself to that love, the more you will find coincidences clustering in your life. When enough of these coincidences have occurred, you will have sufficient courage to let go. When you let go is up to you. If you take a long time to let go you are not a bad channel. If you open up right away you are not necessarily a good channel. If letting go is something you do very easily, then you probably need to work harder on tuning and challenging than you do on getting the contact. If you are having trouble getting your contact, stick with it. It just takes you longer to learn than other people. It took me two months, working every day, before I was able to deliver my first channeled message. It went as follows: "I am Hatonn. Greetings in the love and light of the Infinite Creator. I am having difficulty with this instrument." If I can channel, just about anyone can!

There are things which need to be put in place if you wish to learn to channel. Your biggest need is for a teacher. The teacher may not be that much better than you. What a teacher is, mostly, is more experienced. Those who have been working with the blending of energies between people or between spirits have battle scars after a while; their instincts are much improved from when they began; and perhaps a sense of humor has even been established where before there might have been an overly serious attitude.

The most important requirement for a teacher, in my opinion, is that the teacher be there. NEVER WORK ON CHANNELING BY YOURSELF. Try to make your mistakes in the company of fellow meditators, at least one of which is an experienced channel who feels responsible to you. It's a crowded universe, and the new channel may well not have tuning or the challenging of spirits well learned. You do not really want to tangle with a difficult contact by yourself at first. Things can happen and have happened in the past which caused the hapless channel considerable grief. Consider the public humiliation, for instance, of any woman who announces that she has been told that she will bear the incarnation of Jesus Christ only to be noticeably un-pregnant six months later, or the rueful grin of one who makes a terrifying prediction of certain doom for a certain day, changes his circumstances to a great extent in order to prepare for this dread date and then sees it come and go without incident. These examples only offer embarrassment, which is bad enough—not nearly as bad as another possibility: being repeatedly troubled by a negative entity who, having discovered you, has no desire to stay away.

Often, teachers of meditation and channeling will have groups built up around themselves. If you do not have the luxury of a group, start talking to your friends, if you are a person with a good many like-minded cohorts. If you are a man or woman who has up until recently led a very conventional life, with interests in the usual consumer items such as food, fashions and amusements, but now are taking a great departure from convention and opening up the inner life, you may not have much luck with your friends. In that case it is often fruitful to put a notice about forming a meditation group in the nearest library, health food store, Unitarian or New Age church, or even in the newspaper. Once you have found or formed a group it is ever easier from that point on to add teachers as needed.

Everything that has been covered is part of what you need—I could say review the book again, up until this point, to make sure you have all that you need to channel. However, under the best of circumstances, with a minimum of three in a group, with an experienced channel who is motivated to teach you, with the best of intentions, you still need the peace which only meditation can bring and which only discipline can make stick in your life.

Forgive me for shying away from describing to you one of my actual training sessions. I do not want to make it easy for you to use this book in order to learn to channel by yourself. I worked as a librarian for years and love everything that record-keeping and retrieval implies about the human capacity for learning and creating new things. But it still seems to be the case that some things really shouldn't be available—the plans for a do-it-yourself atom bomb, and the instructions for precipitating spirit contact are two pieces of information I would just as soon not have readily available. If I taught you in these pages how to channel—and I could—I would, by my own code of honor/duty, be responsible for being available to each and every reader as a teacher thereafter. Since that is not possible, I prefer to teach only those who correspond with our group and come to a decision to embark with us on this experience of adventure and service in person.

CHAPTER SIX
TEMPTATIONS

We would all like to think that there are no such things as temptations. It would make life easier, for the nature of temptation is such that often we do not recognize what is happening when a temptation is skewing our judgment or perception of a situation. However, as a responsible channel you are a polarized person, a committed seeker who has a clear personal metaphysic and ethic. You offer yourself wholeheartedly in the service of the general spiritual and philosophical point of view, and, therefore, will be privy to many temptations to act athwart of that stance.

Polarity does not equal a passion for the polarized point of view, but it does imply it. When you behave in a polarized fashion it is logical to assume that you are to some extent attached to the outcome of what you are doing. If it is a speech, you are attached to the outcome of being understood. If it is channeling you are dedicated to the messages' being inspirational. Unless you work on your balance every day, YOU will find your point of view being skewed frequently by the temptations of attachment to outcome. When you know people very well it is especially difficult not to be able to communicate your point of view. The miscommunications that always occur almost inevitably will bring up negative emotions, which can only be balanced on a daily basis, as close to the event of imbalance as possible. The overly-zealous "I can prove it" mentality is typical of the faithful and committed philosopher or metaphysicist, and the spectre of religious twosomes flogging pamphlets door-to-door haunts each of us as we move along our spiritual path attempting to avoid temptations.

I've written already about the importance of straightening out blockages and problems we have in our relationships. After you begin channeling you will find that the extent and intensity of the temptations with which you must deal are linked directly with how troubled and blocked the red, orange and yellow-ray energy centers are. Any advocate's position will by its very nature leave a dynamic vacuum which attracts its counterpoint. Thesis calls antithesis into being. Anything that is not internally balanced within you in mind, body and spirit is fair game for temptation. It is well to work every day on balance as well as on polarity. One tool for working on both of these things is (surprise) meditation, though polarity is probably better worked on by the intuitive mind, in deep and silent meditation and in prayer, whereas one's power of analysis may usefully be brought to bear on questions of internal balance. Each day as you enter meditation, or are leaving it for the night, look back over your day, and when you perceive that there has been an imbalance in your day—say you have been very impatient with a person—you return in mind to that situation, feeling again the intense impatience you felt earlier. Then, take the time to allow the antithesis of impatience, patience, to fill your mind gradually, replacing impatience in a natural flow. Then accept that patience as being part of your earlier impatience, and forgive both yourself and the person with whom you were so impatient for the incident, seeing it as a balanced act rather than an imbalanced one. As of that moment, your bad opinion of that person has been rescinded, and you no longer have the temptation of judging that person in a biased manner.

Temptations which affect channels are usually problems of excess or ego. The red-ray energy center, or the root chakra as it is sometimes called, is the seat of appetite and desire. If you find yourself reacting to the stresses of channeling by overeating, talking too much, indulging too much in alcohol or any other such indulgence of appetites which seems excessive, you are either expressing a blockage of the red-ray center, in which case you need to get in touch with your body and get it to begin feeding you accurate signals, or an orange-ray blockage which has caused disturbance against which you are shielding, in which case you need to re-read the material on getting peaceful. (One other cause of indulging among channels is the need for earth-heavy food while channeling high energies. If you are losing weight while eating normally, you'll need to eat meat, the redder and rarer the better. Sorry.)

Temptations of excess are not the worst that you will ever face as a channel, but if you are dealing with these temptations and failing, it may be that you need to practice moderation in order to have that behavior in place when dealing with orange and yellow-ray blockages, which many people call ego-problems. Although it would be difficult to name all of the signs of the overly large ego in a channel, I can point out some of the bigger categories for you, and you can draw your own conclusions about anything that is not covered here.

Excluding people who don't think as you do is using ego instead of compassion to relate to other people. The notion that you have something that everyone will find as helpful as you do is to be avoided at all costs, and I believe this even speaking as a committed and most grateful Christian. I have seen conversions, but I have only seen them occur when the time was right and when the witness was requested. It is difficult to walk around with answers and not expect everyone's questions to match them. But I have never seen any justification for this frame of mind, because everyone's question is somewhat different in shape, even though we all want to know precisely the same truth. The problems of clouded perception are almost infinitely subtle. Thus, thinking that you have the answers is incorrect thinking in my book. However, many people go through their lives with a relatively narrow point of view, and are extremely good, giving and productive people, because the view that they embrace is one that is held by a satisfactorily great number of other people in the same community. The simpler the social structure, the more this is true. This is why people who have lived long in the country may well find far more things unacceptable than people who live in a big city, and have for a significant portion of their lives. Living with a crush of other people nearby teaches one quickly that almost no one thinks as you do. It is a sobering thought for many, and it probably has a lot to do with the popular resurgence of a simpler form of Christianity in this country, because a lot of people do not want to have to be that broad-minded—it is comfortable to have things spelled out: what to believe, what to think, what to do. Although living by the law is not something that has ever been shown to work, since people always break laws, it is one of the great temptations for people who would prefer not to think. Try to be a little better than the narrow-minded people who condemn those who do not think as they do. Withhold judgment and listen to what people have to say regardless of what it is.

Things that make your channeling sound better are a great temptation, especially to the beginning channel. The great glut of specific information involving cataclysms that are just waiting in the wings is due to the quite logical demand for this kind of information. Say that you get a good philosophical source and are putting out a lot of inspiring material. You receive something about the coming of the New Age. People immediately want to question that. They want to know when it is all going to happen and whether in the birth of that New Age any part of their particular geographical vicinity is going to be made unlivable. People want to be able to survive the cataclysm of the ending of this age, if there's such in store, so that they can enjoy the age to come. Being within the illusion, we all ask questions of our contacts based on the premise that we will have to be living incarnate in a physical body on this planet in order to be able to enjoy the coming age. We forget about the incredible ease of dropping a body and picking up another one. We forget about the logical shape and rhythm of life and death and we want to hang onto this life, regardless of the rightness of the destiny we have programmed for ourselves through the use of our own desires and experiences.

One confusing cross-over which makes egoic temptations more difficult to detect is that the process of choosing what you believe, what you would die for, and, therefore, what you are going to live for makes you a more powerful person. The manipulation of your channeling makes you *feel* more powerful than you are, as does any situation in which you're telling another person what is what. If you like being a more powerful person, you may at first deem it a positive thing to *feel* more powerful, as well, not realizing you can fool yourself. The passionately opinionated person is always more powerful than the disinterested one, simply because the advocate has a motivation for saying something, while the truly disinterested person is likely to go his own way without bothering to set anyone straight, from his point of view. However, when the temptations of ego hit, it will still *feel* as if you are becoming more powerful, when actually you are attempting to create, or half-create, your channeling for the consumption of the audience, which is a no-no! People are always going to want more and more specific information. It is possible that they will want information too specific for your contact to provide on a regular basis. Let's look at that a little bit.

You know that I feel that free will has supremacy as being of the greatest ethical value after the acknowledgment of consciousness itself. I find love an acceptable substitute for the word "consciousness". However, free will is a more important thing to me, when deciding whether or not to do something, than considerations of love. If I am going to infringe on someone's free will by what I say or do, I have to ask myself what right I have to intrude. I have the right to influence my family, my friends, perhaps even my neighbors, if there is some public wrong that needs righting that comes to my attention. Because I am an inhabitant of planet Earth, I have a right to influence others.

However, entities whom I may contact are not inhabitants of planet Earth unless they are discarnate entities who used to live here. Oddly enough, many people do not believe ghosts exist. I've seen quite a few, and will testify as to their apparent reality within my illusion. If you are channeling a ghost, which you well may be doing if you are working with a Spiritualist tradition, the ghost may give specific information, and it may well be that your contact is reliable and that the information will not disintegrate over a period of time, for ghosts are indeed inhabitants of this planet and do have the right to influence others here. If your contact is not a ghost, and you are still getting specific information, beware. The "good guys" abide by the Law of Free Will to an amazing degree, pretty much out of necessity. Part of their desire to be of service is reflected in an attitude so polarized toward service that it is literally impossible for an entity to intrude more than a certain amount on any other entity's free will. Proof is not at any time attempted by metaphysical channels, since each must be free to make each and every choice concerning what to believe and how to live, for himself. However, negative contacts are very happy to give polluted information, polluted in the sense that the original positive message has been taken and edited so as to include additional information, which may or may not be true, but which is by its very nature going to depolarize the contact, making it gradually more negative and less positive, until the balance turns and the light which you have begun generating by acting in a polarized manner in service to the Creator goes out. To avoid that just keep looking for the highest and most informed contact and know that that contact will be unwilling and even unable to violate the dictates of free will. And so be warned when you begin to get an excessive amount of specific information.

Your group, given that you are already channeling for a group, may well want specific information whether you want to channel it or not. If your chosen field of channeling is outer-plane, a "cosmic" contact rather than an inner-planes master, teacher or other discarnate but once embodied spirit, you may have to set group policy and say "No specific questions, please." If you wish not to limit people's imaginations by such a blanket disclaimer, you may simply allow yourself to sound silly fairly often, as you channel the explanation that you cannot answer that particular question because it would be an infringement on free will. We are talking about temptation, and the temptation to supply information that is requested is one of the trickier egoic temptations. You really want your channeling to be good, and to be received as good. One doesn't like to be criticized, and when all one has got for one's pains is a series of "I can't tell you, because it would violate free will," the listener may be somewhat less than stunned by the excellence of your channeling. I advise you to live with that! The potential of giving in to this kind of temptation is the end of your contact and of your use as an instrument by positive contacts.

It is a temptation to stay with one of the great misconceptions of every new channel, and that is that it is not really happening. The activity of telepathic reception has been studied, and one day will be documented, I am sure. But for now, our instrumentation is not enough sophisticated for the reliable documentation of this activity. When you begin to channel, it is inevitable that you will think that you are the author of everything that you say, that there's a great conspiracy of people who are pretending that channeling is real when, of course, it isn't real. As each new channel gains experience, the subjective case for the source of information as being outside of the waking consciousness gets more and more persuasive until finally the channel no longer has very many qualms about working in any situation where the atmosphere and environment seem conducive to a peaceful session. However, the unconscious assumption that it really isn't happening somehow remains at the bottom of every channel's mind and when a difficult question comes up the channel will tend to search his own knowledge, his own stores of accumulated conscious lore for the answer instead of leaving the mind free for whatever may come through. The longer that you have been channeling, the less excuse you have for this kind of lack of discipline, for the more confident you should be in the reality of what you are experiencing as an instrument.

If you fall into the category of one who truly believes that one is generating one's own material rather than channeling it, I would like to know why you are reading this book, and why you are interested in channeling. It is true that it is easier to separate people from their money when they think that they're paying you to function as a channel than when they think they are paying for your advice. People often underrate good advice and overrate religiously oriented pronouncements, not trusting in their own powers of discrimination but rather in the power of someone else to know what is best, if that person is a religious or spiritual figure. Now, I really think that if you are reading these words, there is something in you that is saying the phenomenon is real. It has been a real experience to me and, I think, to many others.

Try not to give in to the temptation to answer in your own words or in any way misuse the power of channeling. If you receive nothing, channel nothing. Every once in a while this will happen to you. Think of it as a test. If you are committed to your point of view you will not use your channeling ability in the service of a lesser ideal than your highest and best. If it is more important to you to produce something for your group than to channel well, channeling is not your area; being an instrument is not your forte. Turn instead to something over which you have complete control, at least in the sense of all your tools' being in the world of objects. A typical social worker, for instance, must fight a great deal of red tape, ingrained behavior patterns and the emotional biases of many people in order to be of service, but at least he or she does not have to depend on unseen and invisible emanations which are available only unpredictably. An instrument works closely with uncontrolled energies; that is, energies not under the conscious control of your waking personality. Always look at your personality and at the personality of each student, as you set about the work of channeling, for if you are not comfortable with the concept of being overshadowed by a force greater than you, or at least other and different than you, you will be miserable as a channel, and you will undoubtedly find the temptation of using your own information to the exclusion of awaiting the unpredictable contact too much to bear.

People are often all too easy to impress, right now anyway, channeling for the last several years having come into fashion. While it is chic, people that wish to experience everything that is out there to experience will be listening to anything that claims to be channeled information with an uncritical ear, curious and eager to learn more. If a person of whom you think a lot asks you a question to which your contact does not reply it is very easy to fall off the channeling wagon and give your own opinion as part of the channeled message. You can say to yourself that you are actually just saying what the contact would say if you were channeling and, therefore, are not misleading anyone. This isn't true. If someone's opinion is more important to you than your own knowledge that you have channeled honestly, again, you should be in a line of work in which you do not have to depend on unseen friends whose situation you cannot control. If someone whom you do not know asks you a personal question, you will likely not know the answer. The human temptation is to give the ego a little bit of room and make a comment that would indicate neither that you knew or did not know the information, but did indicate an appropriate attitude. It's called saving face. Tell it as it is, to yourself and to everyone else. People have only your word that you are channeling at all, much less producing material in good faith from the best source you can contact. This whole business can be a con game, because a confidence game is based on other people's trust whether you deserve it or not. Don't be a con man. Deserve the trust that people will inevitably put in you. You're not responsible for the information itself but only for the production of that information, by your preparation as an instrument of integrity, by the tuning you have undergone and the challenges you make before you accept contact. Think of yourself as the village philosopher, if you want a handy slot in which to put yourself. That philosopher has often been a drunk and when not a drunk, often an idiot. You are merely upholding a long-standing tradition of people whose minds have been upset and overshadowed by a force greater than their own, obviously rather weak minds. Let your mind be called anything, but let your faith in the overshadowing of a benign and kindly universe capable of communicating to us furnish you with enthusiasm and respect for the channeling that you have set out to do.

Here is a situation for you: you start getting information from a Lord Joseph, or a Commander Umgawa. You know that names of contacts are often somewhat similar to the sounds that young children make when they are trying out the language—lots of exotic consonants and a liberal supply of vowels. The title may not at first mean anything to you. Be warned. The title is a kind of temptation; a name that makes your channeling seem better serves to aid the perceived elevation of the contact. Mind you, this is not something you have consciously done. In part you are responding to childhood training perhaps, a childhood in which a Jewish or Christian service you attended filled your ears full of Lords and titles such as Almighty, Everlasting, Blessed, Holy, Omniscient, Omnipresent and Wonderful. It sounds natural to have Lord Hatonn, for instance, instead of Hatonn in terms of spiritual talk that you have heard previously. Also a factor is the inevitable respect which you will develop for your contact or contacts, causing you unconsciously to give them honor in your own mind. However, it has not been my experience that it is common for even the most far-advanced positively polarized spiritual entity to offer praise on its own behalf or use a title. The typical contact is attempting to get out of the way of the message itself which the contact considers its only reason for communication. Contacts do seem to take an almost childlike delight in meeting with the people who sit in a session or in meditation. However, they make note of their delight by blessing those whom they have met, not by talking about their titles and honors. When you hear such a title, as you inevitably will, challenge the contact again in the name of the highest and best that you know. Lesser contacts flee from you if you ally yourself with a matchless point of view with every fiber of your being. Mind you, there may yet be an entity who is Lord this or Commander that, who happens to be a good source of very interesting information. Your contact may be the exception I have not yet run across. However, the odds are against it.

The final temptation is a simple one, and I have talked about it already: the temptation to progress too fast. Try to remember at all times that what you are working on is basically not your channeling but yourself. It is yourself that you bring to channeling, and only yourself. All your work is interior.

All your advances are invisible. You are disciplining your mind and your personality in order that it might be turned over to the highest and best source that you can contact for purposes of information giving. If you attempt to add phenomena to your little list of achievements too quickly, while disregarding and not dealing with the matters and concerns of daily life, you may well cause a real weakness in your being by allowing blockages in the lower energy centers to occur, severely limiting the amount of light that is available for use by the heart chakra. Respect yourself enough to *be* yourself, whatever the temptation to improve artificially or beforehand upon the person you truly are, right now.

CHAPTER SEVEN
PSYCHIC GREETING

A lot has been written about psychic attack. I prefer to call it psychic greeting, since the shift in attitude is the key to dealing with this occurrence. How many times have you heard a news commentator report that a psychotic killer has claimed he heard a voice telling him to kill? How many movies have had as their subject the possession of a soul by an outside force? Roman Catholic literature has a fairly substantial supply of books on possession by demons or by Satan himself. Anyone who has ever witnessed a sustained psychic greeting upon someone else or himself is fully aware of the reality of the occurrence. If you are reading this book, whatever your previous opinion of psychic greeting, I say to you as a potential or working channel that this is part of the vocation you have elected to pursue.

Anything that we do within this lifetime may be looked at as a kind of game. If we are working on our own maturity, we have begun making up our own rules, choosing what we believe and fashioning the game to suit our biases and choices. Being an instrument makes you a player in a game where all the pieces are invisible and have to do with feeling and faith. There are many presences in our invisible universe, many more by far than we can see as we go about our daily life. We do well to choose our point of view carefully and stick with it faithfully in order that we may have the most fastidious choice of contacts, aligning ourselves with the highest and best thought we can.

We then offer ourselves for a kind of positive possession or partial possession. Any channel who is relaying a message has opened itself to what is intended to be just that. Through tuning and challenging of spirits the contact itself is safeguarded. However, just because you have tuned and challenged during meditation, it does not follow that you are in a centered and focused frame of mind later that same day or the next morning. The channel, in playing the game of being an instrument for inspiration, plays a role that is intended to be larger than life, in that the focusing and polarizing is centered upon being a far better instrument than one normally is in a steady state of consciousness. My consciousness, as I am writing on tape for you this morning, is not the same consciousness I possessed in the bathroom earlier when I rather abruptly moved my cat, Freeway, from his precarious three-legged posture (he lost one limb as a little kitten) atop the sink I wished to use at that moment. The third time he crawled into it he went down faster than he came up. That bad temper is the kind of opening which makes one vulnerable to psychic greeting.

There are other forms of psychic greeting, besides the classic feeling of being possessed by another mind. There are times, for instance, when one's best intentions are lost in an amazing flurry of bad luck at a critical time. Opportunities can be cut off that will never come again. If a person runs into these things randomly it is undoubtedly the working of happenstance. It does not do to get paranoid; unfortunate coincidences are far more frequent occurrences than are psychic greetings. However, if you have been experiencing a lot of polarizing changes of consciousness lately, and because of those changes of consciousness find yourself wishing to do something for someone else that would be noteworthy in some way, you may not be paranoid by ascribing bad luck to more than simple coincidence. When you begin attempting to polarize yourself you may find after a few weeks, months or years that you have done enough work to experience the time of transformation which is sometimes called initiation. I have experienced two of them of which I am aware; there may have been more which were hidden from me by the mundane nature of crisis: I have often thought that initiations sometimes take place through the catalyst of illness or tragedy, when the biocomputer-mind is full of the energy of dumped programs.

During initiation one can get very uncomfortable. One tends to lose sleep and experience unwelcome and seemingly negative greeting. The initiatory period may last two months or two years. There is a period to any initiation, a merciful ending of the stimulus once it is no longer needed. The phenomenon, in my opinion, has to do with the "lions at the gates of the temple" concept which has been related to me by Buddhist students. When one moves from one level of intensity of seeking or adoration to another, one is changing one's basic level of consciousness, and in order to move from one level to the next, one must move through a semipermeable boundary area. There is resistance at the boundary, making it more difficult to make the shift than to stay where one is. The process of initiation involves a steadfastness of seeking and a confidence that all is truly well in spite of appearances, that love will indeed conquer all.

The most common experiences during this kind of transformational period are nightmares which wake one up with regularity in the deep of night, with the most likely period of awakening being from three-thirty to four in the morning if you have a normal sleeping pattern. During the day the feelings of nightmare—baseless unease and dread—can continue with or without waking nightmare visions. One can get stray negative thoughts which, seemingly, coming from nowhere, immediately take over the mind, challenging the stability and courage of the seeker. There can be the intensification of any existing physical disease or unease, or mental or emotional unease. My bad temper at the cat's importunities is one opening which a negatively oriented spirit could use to trigger feelings of guilt in me—for indeed I should have been more patient not just then, but in other situations throughout my life. Anything one does that is unbalanced like that, ungraceful, disharmonious, petty, is a freely-given hostage taken by the forces which wish to block the positive work that you are doing. If you pay attention to the sounds inside your mind—most seekers and students whom I have known have experienced these—you may find one sound or position of sound in the head which will serve as a warning when something erroneous is being thought, or may serve as a signal when you are doing something extremely well for the first time, and the thought is one which you wish to emphasize and remember.

When most people come to me with questions about psychic greeting, the thrust of their inquiry is as much, "Why me?" as "What is it?" The why's of psychic greetings begin with the already noted orientation of the instrument toward the invisible world. Channels are committed to service to others by communication with unseen sources. If you are an instrument whose work is generating positive emotions and thoughts in those whom the words are serving, you are functioning as a messenger for a source of light, light that is invisible to most of our waking eyes but is all-powerful in the world of thought.

Let me put the concept of Armageddon before you because I believe that there is a kind of Armageddon that has been on-going for quite a long time on the inner planes. What I am telling you is my opinion only, and I do not wish to sway you by it, but this is what I think the nature of Armageddon really is: I believe that consciousness exists in several densities or levels of awareness. Earth, wind, water and fire are of the first density; plants, animals and all things that grow are of the second-density; and self-conscious, third-density beings take up a more 'spiritualized' or light-filled body, with light packed more densely, hence the term, 'density.' Fourth-density entities are completing the lessons of love and beginning the attempt to learn wisdom in addition to love. Because real love is the Creator, agent and enabler of service to others, fourth-density beings have a strong desire to protect those of third-density—us—from the massive amount of information made available to us by their opposite numbers—

fourth-density negatively polarized beings, who have the reciprocal attitude toward fourth-density *positively* polarized beings. The concept of angels and demons in a heavenly battle is not an altogether satisfactory distortion of what I conceive the situation to be, but it is recognizable as the same situation. I do believe that one era or density is coming to an end on planet Earth and that another is about to begin. I don't believe that there is any necessity for a totally catastrophic earth change or changes, although I have read some of the same books you may have and accept the possibility, in some cases even the probability, of some inconvenience, as my favorite contact once called the probable scenario of earth changes. While we move through the process of density change the Armageddon of the thought world rages. Neither side can win because the forces of love lose polarity by doing battle and as they begin to win, as they must, since they bear the standard of love, they realize that they must pull back in order to regain polarity. In leaving the field of battle they lose the edge that they have gained. And so the battle is unending. It is my somewhat sad conclusion that this is a war that will not end in any probable future. However, the negative polarity is valuable, and needs to be appreciated. Without the concept of polarity there would be no way to accelerate the process of spiritual evolution, either in the path of service to others, or unity, or in the path of service to self, or separation.

We are talking as instruments, for the most part, to those of the next density, occasionally fifth or sixth density, but more often fourth, who are in some way involved in this spiritual Armageddon. It is not a battle in which spirits are slain; it is a battle for minds and hearts. When you accept the responsibility of becoming a contact for a positively oriented source of information you are joining this battle. And because you are working for the forces of light—by definition, not making a judgment between good and evil—you are, by connection, vulnerable to the same attacks from what could be called enemy forces, though because we are sources of light the last thing we wish to do is hate, fear or feel anger towards negatively oriented, unseen beings.

When you have generated a significant amount of light by yourself or within a group, you will probably be greeted by those on the negative path. The closer you have managed to bring your life and your work to the consciousness of the source of all love and light, the fiercer will be the greeting offered to you. This is part of the plan, I believe, of a fair-minded Creator who believes that the free-will choices of His creations are far more effective than the relatively uninteresting actions of those who do not have a choice but who must be good, or evil. So if you are, or think you are, receiving a psychic greeting, do not ask, "Why me?" for everything that you have done to prepare yourself to be a channel, and all that you do to be faithful in service as an instrument, has put you in an extremely predictable situation: you will come to the attention of those lobbying for the antithetical point of view to the one offered by messengers of love, light and service to others.

"How should I handle it?" you have asked me quite often. "As soon as possible," is the first answer that comes to mind. A psychic greeting is like priority mail. It should get your attention immediately. In the first place you would not be getting a psychic greeting unless you had left yourself open to temptation, had been successfully tempted and did not amend your thought or action, for if you deal with temptations as they arise, psychic greeting is not possible. A person that leaves no openings will not be attacked. If negatively oriented entities could be said to have one predictable characteristic, that characteristic is caution. Negative entities have a great deal to lose if they get into a situation where they will fail. Failing is a negative no-no. Look at the situation from the negative point of view. Service to the self, the controlling of others for the use of the self, is the name of the game. If you cannot control another you have failed, so it is unlikely in the extreme that you are undergoing some type of psychic greeting unless you have left yourself indefensible on some point.

We've talked about some of the temptations, most of which have to do with either ego or excess. Look through your relationships, your conversations and your private behavior for those actions which are not consistent with your own deepest point of view. Because you are in a vulnerable position as an instrument, vis-à-vis psychic greeting, it is well for you to be thinking in terms of ethical behavior so that you do not cause yourself unnecessary difficulties. You may have to force yourself to recognize and accept your own shortcomings. It is far easier to say that you are being attacked by someone or something that hates you because you are a messenger of light than it is to take responsibility for the "attack," recognizing that you have placed yourself in the position in which you now are by some omission or commission of action or thought.

You are not alone if you find yourself wasting time by saying "But I have done nothing." You probably have done very little; however, anything which leaves room for question may be enough to let in negative greeting. The harder that you want to work for light and the more that you want to help this planet, the more care you must take in the conduct of your own private and public thoughts and relationships. It does not matter what anyone else thinks of you, in the spiritual sense. You are not responsible to other people's opinions. If you are acting according to the highest and best that you know in metaphysic and ethic, and if your life equals your thinking and your work, you have eliminated the cause of psychic greeting. Of course if you are human and on the planet in a physical body at this time, you have probably not succeeded in becoming the ideal, God-realized being. Just keep trying.

When you respond to psychic greeting with fear or anger you are giving negatively oriented entities precisely what they want. The more you fear, the more you struggle and the more you rage, the tighter will be their grip upon your attention and the less you will be able to do about their greeting of you. To those upon the negative path, negative emotions are sweet. It may seem backwards to us, but taken in terms of negative polarity fear and anger are quite normal, and the more fear and anger you feel towards a negatively oriented entity, the more that entity feels you have complimented its work.

It is up to you to invoke the power of love in this situation. My favorite contact, a group entity of many individuals called Ra, has called the positive path "the path of that which is" and the negative path "the path of that which is not." Love makes us all one and is all that there is; however, the positive path is based upon an appreciation of that fact, whereas the negative path is based upon a denial of that fact.

Since universal love is the natural environment of the positive polarity it is relatively easily generated, by thinking on the Creator of all that there is, for that original consciousness, undistorted and whole, underlies all that there is—this is the basic belief system of those whose channeled messages we are getting, at least in the majority. Love is delicious to those of positive polarity when it is non-manipulative. However non-manipulative, unconditional love given to negatively polarized beings is as distasteful to them as anger and fear are delicious. All that is good to us is evil to them, for they are perceiving the exact opposite of the path of light. Thus the power of love is not found in its ability to control as much as in its capacity to fill positive things with joy and negative things with the desire to leave. Sending unconditional love to a negative entity who greets you psychically is much like sending a bouquet of spoiled flowers. The smell is malodorous and sickening to the recipient, who promptly turns on his heels and vacates the premises, having realized *it* is the receiver of a positively oriented "psychic greeting."

However, you cannot send love in order that the entity will go away. This is conditional love, and as such is very dear to the hearts of negatively oriented entities. If you wonder about this seeming contradiction, look at relationships where two people are trying to control each other through love. It is never a pretty sight. Control and love are conflicting forces. *Unconditional* love should be sent to the entity which is greeting you. It should then be sent separately and consciously to the greeting itself. Love should also be sent to yourself, that you may have the grace to forgive the intrusion and forget it completely. It is always well to conclude with an inner statement of fidelity to the point of view which you have come to hold and a form of thanksgiving that is meaningful to you, and to the Creator for giving you this opportunity to learn.

If you have gone through a series of experiences of psychic greeting without having the knowledge of how to deal with them this may seem like an extremely oversimplified answer to a thorny problem. It is simple; however, it is also effective. Just remember that the first thing you need at all times is knowledge of yourself so that you may have faith in who you are, be energetically engaged in the pursuit of positive polarity in a way consistent with your point of view and, above all, be committed to service. Once you have your feeling of self well articulated you have positioned yourself in such a way that dealing with psychic greetings becomes a simple application of faith and will. You must have faith in the power of love, you who are servants of the consciousness of love, and you must have the will to use love to respond to a greeting from negative entities. For without willpower there is a great temptation to feel sorry for yourself and powerless in the face of the unseen. If you are not afraid to channel the positive, do not be afraid to face the negative serenely.

There is a difficulty with filling your mind with something immediately after you have gone through psychic greeting and the sending of love. It takes a few minutes, at least, for the feeling of being invaded to fade entirely from the consciousness, whether you have just hallucinated that you have stepped on a small dead animal, or smelled an awful smell which was found to be sourceless or had a waking nightmare which terrified you (all these things have happened to me). I don't want to start listing frightening things that can happen to one undergoing psychic greeting; if you are reading this chapter with interest you probably have a lot to tell me! A history of some encounters I have had with psychic greetings is included in THE LAW OF ONE, Volumes One through Four, especially Volume Three. While you are waiting for this aftertaste to disappear you are still vulnerable even though you have sent love, because fear and anger at the intrusion are still possible. Sometimes the mind does not want to let go of those emotions. It is well to fashion for yourself some general statement of affirmation and have it on hand to say to yourself, preferably out loud, during those five or ten minutes that it takes for you to get back into a comfortable frame of mind. I have written my own, and you may wish to write yours also. Counting your blessings is a good way of expressing the kind of writing I would encourage. You may also use affirmations that have been written by others, such as Psalm 91 or Psalm 23.

If you are waking up in the middle of the night and have trouble getting back to sleep because of psychic greeting coming to you through nightmares, you may find a prayer of Dion Fortune's helpful and I would encourage you to read her book, PSYCHIC SELF-DEFENSE, now available in paperback. If you are a member of a group which is undergoing greeting from a negative source and your place of working has been compromised, I recommend W. E. Butler's book. THE MAGICIAN: HIS TRAINING AND WORK, also available in paperback. Fortune's book is written from the standpoint of Christ-consciousness' being an expression of perfect love. Both books are written by practicing white magicians. I do recommend this additional reading, since these authors give not only solutions that work but also an excellent foundation for removing the feeling of strangeness from the situation. It is not a good idea to be in awe of negative forces, nor is it good to be flippant about them, but rather to be in balance and to be able to respond appropriately using the polarity you have gained and asking for the forces of light to aid you. The books may or may not be what you are looking for; however, I feel it would be irresponsible of me to tell you about the very helpful material in them without recommending the volumes in *toto*.

The practice of ritual magic is demanding and should not be undertaken by yourself alone, or lightly. However, some few specific applications of ritual are benign and helpful even to novices. Don Elkins, Jim McCarty and I used material from these volumes during our contact with the social memory complex of Ra and found it to be efficacious and most uplifting to us all personally as well. It is work done with devotion or not at all, and I hope you will take it most seriously if you decide to pursue this material. Further, I would greatly appreciate you doing your reading *before* you use any material. It is important in the context of their contribution to ritual magic and their making this material available that the student who essays its use read what else the authors had to offer.

As a channel you are a bridge from the world of thought to the world of what we see around us. Try in all things to lend your frame of mind to respect and honor the invisible world, both its positive and its negative citizens. All are denizens of the same creation and unique and precious portions of the One Creator. We share consciousness, and we are all literally in it together. Be not afraid!

Chapter Eight
The Ethics Of Channeling

As in any other endeavor wherein you deal with other people, there needs to be a code of right conduct in channeling that exists for the protection of the feelings of the people with whom you are dealing and of yourself. Although vast amounts of money seldom change hands, people's feelings are often deeply involved in transactions with a channel, and just as others treat you, the instrument, with a good deal of respect, so you respect them and your position.

Money will come to you in the course of your channeling, whether you ask for it or not, if your work has a stable basis of preparation and dedication, and especially if you have made any of your information public. In the Holy Bible, love of money is considered quite nefarious; about money itself, that particular holy work seems to conclude little, except that one should have a sense of stewardship towards the money one does make. It is not unethical, in my opinion, to charge money for serving as an instrument. Many excellent channels do charge and since they spend their working lives acting as instruments at the behest of others it seems only logical that these instruments should be able to make a living. However, anything can be carried too far. The price charged for, say, an hour's session with an instrument varies widely, and it is difficult to say when "enough" has become "too much." Perhaps the most commonsense way to look at charging money for channeling is that if you need to do so in order to channel, and if you feel that you are doing work worthy of accepting payment, you should certainly go ahead and charge. I would advise you to keep your price in line with your experience and effort, and with your actual daily needs. No amount of emolument can pay enough for your dedication, nor should you hope for such. Some channels, for instance, lose a great deal of personal time, not just during channeling sessions but in their aftermath, being frail physically and unable to withstand the rigors of serving in this way particularly well. If you are new, young, inexperienced and healthy, be conservative in the price you charge. As you gain experience, charge more. Remember that like any other professional you are "taking work home" in that when you accept the responsibility of being a channel you are accepting what I would call, with my Christian background, a lay ministry, a ministry by one of the flock, not the shepherd; a ministry by a member of the congregation and not the priest. As a kind of deacon, without dogma or doctrine, but totally dedicated to the service of the Creator as you have come to know Him, and to humankind, you have the responsibility of attempting at all times to place your life in the service of those ideals you have decided are yours. If you are charging money—and even if you are not—be sure you are offering a good value, the best value you can make, of the way you live your life. It is not only what is going on in your head that will ultimately aid others. The life that you live will speak far more loudly to people than any fine thought you might be able to opine or channel.

There is another alternative to charging money: accepting contributions. Because I have been extremely fortunate financially, I have never had to charge for serving as an instrument. Many women can with gratitude say the same thing. I have not ever had an overabundance of this world's goods, but have always had "enough," for myself, if not for this work, and so when I looked for a way to allow people to support my work I found the non-profit corporation, a private or public charity, a desirable option. It is not as easy as it used to be to acquire a 501(c)(3) ruling from the Internal Revenue Service, but it is possible. The corporation, then, is able to pay for printing costs, costs of mailing and other costs which one who attempts to make channeling information available to others must incur.

There are metaphysical points to be made here in favor of not charging. There is a kind of law concerning giving which suggests that charging a certain amount of money for service limits the amount which people can feel free to donate. There is also a money law which has more to do with keeping the green-ray energy center open than with good financial thought: it is impossible for some people to pay for materials which you have channeled; often prisoners cannot pay; many older readers cannot show their appreciation monetarily; youngsters still in school may have an impossibly tight money situation if they are not working. On the other hand, several excellent channels have advised me that I am naive to think that many will listen carefully to me unless I charge enough to get their respect and attention. The argument posits that a student's potential for learning and transformation rises in direct proportion to the size of the fee for your teaching and the sacrifice involved in saving it. It also assumes that what is offered to the student is worth its price. These are considerations, and I hope you will think them through carefully before you decide what to do about charging money.

When it comes to large projects, such as workshops and speaking engagements out of town, money considerations change a bit due to the amount of money which you would be owing if you did not charge something. Again, it is not unethical to charge a fee or a fee plus expenses for speaking or offering a seminar. If you decide to charge a fee, try to make sure it is in the normal range for the time and the services provided. You might also consider whether or not some special people—the elderly, the very poor, the young—might be exempt from normal charges. My policy is this: I'll go anywhere to speak if invited, provided that those who invite me pay my expenses. This puts me in a position where I have not lost anything by teaching. There is more than a bit of selfishness there, but I do live on a budget, like most people, and could not offer to go places were my expenses not covered. However, once I am there, any additional monies collected by whatever group I address are accepted as a contribution, welcome but not expected. What you will find as you continue channeling is that people are very grateful for this kind of work and want to help you. You do not have to be on the lookout for ways to make money. Your main difficulty will be in keeping things in perspective so that you do not find yourself overwhelmed by temptation when someone is willing to pay you a good deal of money in order to hear certain kinds of information which you do not wish to try to channel.

One last word about money: if you are charging money, the acceptance of that fee creates a bond of a contractual nature between you and the person whom you have served. Be careful, therefore, whom you serve. In this crazy day where more money is made in lawsuits, so it seems, than in honest labor, it is well to choose with some care those to whom you will be obligated. This is another reason I personally prefer accepting contributions to charging a set fee.

There is an old gypsy ethic that suggests that fortune tellers never divulge bad news, especially news of someone's upcoming death. It doesn't matter how clear it is in the hand, or how plain the tea leaves are to read, it is just not done. I have heard of very inventive ways of getting around this. For instance there is the case of my friend, Denny, who went to a psychic. She acted disturbed, and among other things, told him never to accept a ride in a red car. Quite a while later Denny was hitchhiking. He was picked up by a red VW beetle, which crashed horrendously. Denny almost didn't make it back to this earth plane, and when he did he was to have a long, slow pull back to health, as he had suffered brain damage. He is fine now, but will never be as he was before. It is too bad that he did not remember to avoid maroon automobiles, but on the other hand, news of this death would have disturbed him perhaps more in mind than in its actual near-occurrence. In the same situation, try just as hard to find ways of channeling which circumnavigate prophesy.

If you are naturally gifted as a psychic as well as functioning as a channel you may have no choice about what you perceive. You may get a flood of information that you don't necessarily want to have. Nevertheless, because you are gifted and are receiving it, you are also responsible for using it correctly. Try in what you say to inspire people, not just with your channeling but in those things which you share person to person. Try for the "beware of red cars" technique rather than either a bald statement like "You are going to die," or refraining from saying anything at all. Use both common sense and whatever faculty of intuition and prayer may be yours. Common sense is the more sturdy of the two faculties for this kind of discrimination; however, some calls are too close to make using logic alone.

Channels who have had success over a period of time doing good work can often run into ethical difficulty by allowing people to become dependent on them. Try not to do this with your own practice. Remember that you are here to serve others. They did not show up in order to serve you. Regardless of who does what to whom, your attitude should remain one of open-hearted and compassionate service. Thus you need continuously to make distinction between what you say as yourself and what your contact says through you as a channel. If you have tuned carefully and challenged all entities who come before your notice, the contact which you ultimately obtain will be of positive polarity and will not attempt to make people dependent on it.

If your contact is channeling things through you which are making people dependent on it and you, you need to rethink your channeling. Ask yourself if you have a really sound and stable dedication to serving through the practice of channeling. Ask yourself what the shape of that commitment is and how you can improve your challenging and tuning processes to prepare yourself to receive a higher and better contact. If you have spotted channeling that seems to be going in the direction of making people come back and back in order to get something they feel they need, do not put this matter from your mind until you have assured yourself that nothing you are doing is in any way tying this person to you or to the contact. Some people are naturally dependent, and there is nothing you should do about that. However, if you are not channeling specific information but rather offering metaphysical and philosophical inspiration, you should consider yourself to be on the right track regardless of the number of hangers-on you may have accumulated over the years, remembering always that most of your students and readers will come back for years, perhaps, with the best and most inner-directed motives. There's a big difference between those inquiring spirits who make up a channel's audience and the occasional clinging vines who don't like to think, especially for themselves.

There is no one sure merciful way to discourage naturally dependent seekers from attaching themselves to you. As long as you avoid being self-serving and channeling specific prophecy you will not offer the kind of naturally tempting environment which will keep hangers-on hanging on! Examine your behavior to be sure that you are not encouraging this sort of channeling in order to feed your ego. People will seek at their own speed and along their own path of inquiry. The answers important to them will be awakened from within them, not from outside of them, through a process of recognition of truth that is impossible to describe but which almost everyone has experienced. You are not responsible to anyone except insofar as you are living as well as you can in accordance with what you believe and are channeling in a responsible and dedicated fashion.

Once you have been serving in this capacity for a while you will start to discover your time disappearing, if indeed you had any left over in the first place. People begin calling you up from around areas in which you have spoken, wanting to know more about your work. If you have a published a book, readership eventually becomes a matter of national circulation, then international circulation, and one day you are dealing with people who have never read English. Everyone wants you to write to them or speak to their organization and yet there is just so much you can do in any day's time. What are your ethical responsibilities? Do you need to make yourself available to the public?

It is my opinion that you do. You do not have to carry it too far, or give over your life, your home and your work to the business of being with people. If you do that, you will find that you have also stopped being an instrument. You need to allow yourself solitude for meditation, contemplation, reading, goofing off and having a ball. These are all highly constructive activities which make the instrument far more able to focus and concentrate during the next work period. However, it is important to make yourself available to people. So how is it done?

One of the easiest and best ways I know to share yourself with people is to put aside a certain day each week, or each fortnight or month if such be your scheduling needs, for the public. Our group, for instance, has had a

Sunday night meditation almost every week since January, 1962, with the meetings being at my house since 1974. With this time already set aside it is far more possible to handle requests from people who want to come see you. You simply tell them the day and time of your weekly open-house and invite them to it. Although this is a time-consuming way of handling your obligations, it is also a time-saving method insofar as you have accumulated all of your debts to those whom you serve into one time-period per week. To the extent that you feel responsible for making extra dates with out-of-towners and strangers at times other than that one day, this plan will be a failure. If you are setting aside a specific time for this responsibility to be discharged, you owe it to yourself and your work to try to keep your time with the public limited to that day and time.

People are wonderful and I could probably spend all my time just talking and being with folks. However, my Puritan background must still hold a great deal of sway with me because I persist having the illusion that there is something more for me to do than chat, however charming or meaningful the conversation. If you are tremendously enjoying meeting lots of different people, go ahead and do it. It is likely that the experience itself will sate you and once you have gotten your fill of people you will be far more able to temper your enthusiasm with a little respect for your other needs. You really do owe all the people whom you are serving a chance to ask anything that they want to ask, to share anything that they want to share. You are not, however, responsible for doing that at their convenience but rather for making the effort at all. People who say "I will only be in town for one day and I must see you," no longer tug at my heartstrings as they once did, because I have sat through far too many conversations where the people talked to me for hours at a time very inconvenient to me. It seems that at least half of the people who "absolutely must see you" at an awkward time are people who want to change you or to use you as a sounding board for something outside your field of inquiry, and while I do not mind listening to criticism or being sympathetic if I have the time, I don't think any instrument has the responsibility of taking the time away from his or her own private life to do this.

If you have published any of your channeling, and many instruments have, you will begin getting letters from people, some good, some bizarre, some merely sad. This correspondence represents an ethical commitment which I would encourage you to undertake, to the balancing of any energy that wants to blend with yours. A letter is a far more grateful medium for sharing opinion than a personal visit because the etiquette of face-to-face discussions is such that you may well find yourself too embarrassed or polite to offer the appropriate opinion and thus blunt your words because of courtesy. In a letter both praise and blame can be tempered with compassion in a far more careful and thoughtful way than is available to someone face to face with another, since a letter can be written and rewritten and sent out only after you are completely satisfied with the degree of compassion that it shows. When you are talking you only have one chance per thought. People who send you letters are sending you energy just as much as people who come to visit you. To discharge your responsibilities to them it is well to blend your energy with theirs in as compassionate and loving a way as is possible. It is not always possible to get very close to people. More than once in my life I have been very sad to notice the great gap that exists between the close friendship that can be achieved in letters and the uneasy comradeship that can ensue in person if two people are communicating in two widely various ways with each other. I have wished, in fact, that we communicated through the equivalent of a letter at all times! We do so much better. So answer every letter if you can. We do.

After trying to devise a telephone ethic for several years, I personally elected to take an unpublished number and filter all calls through our telephone answering device. People who hate answering machines virtually never contact me by telephone. This is my response to telephone tyranny. It you have a listed number, be prepared for frequent incursions on your time at all hours by strangers. You're on your own on this subject, as I dislike telephones to the exclusion of a rational ethic!

A discussion of the ethics of channeling wouldn't be complete without talking about confidentiality. I'm talking to two different kinds of channels here, and so I will need to ask you a question. Are you a priest or a lay person? Quite a few channels are actually priests, having incorporated as a church or monastery, and having set up a way of ordaining ministers in that church. The rule of confidentiality of the priesthood is absolute. A priest does not have to go to jail for refusing to divulge to a court the confessions of a criminal. That professional ethic extends to psychiatrists, who have the equivalent of a priesthood conferred on them by the scientific community and public opinion in general. You, however, are probably not legally a priest and, as a lay minister, are as responsible to the forces of justice as you are the confidentiality of the confessional. I believe you can play it either way. However, it would be well to think this one through before the situation comes up. If you agree to hear the confidences of a person who, it turns out, has done or seen something relevant to a crime, you will have to make a response to that situation, either by calling on the ethics of confidentiality or by telling the officer of the court to which you are responsible what you know. This is a decision you will have to make for yourself. It is a gray area, in my opinion. I lean towards absolute confidentiality; however, I know that that opinion could put me in jail one day. It is simply my experience that in this illusion the forces of loyalty have a deeper metaphysical meaning than the forces of mundane justice. And, of course, each case needs to be judged, to a certain extent, on its own merits.

Back to money and taxation! It is a great temptation, if you are not already putting contributions in a special non-profit account which you cannot personally touch, to pocket whatever cash may be given to you as a contribution without making any kind of record of the income. I am not fond of the IRS. I may be crazy, but I am not that crazy! However, it is an unfortunate fact that the way one lives one's life is always relevant to the work one does as a channel. Therefore, as an instrument you would do well to be painfully and expensively honest. Keep careful books and pay what you owe. Hopefully that will not be a death knell to your service. However, it would, in my opinion, be better to stop taking money for your work than to pocket it as undeclared income.

You are going to be asked an enormous number of questions if you continue channeling and teaching channeling for any length of time. Some of the questions will be repeated over and over again, but there are always questions that surprise you, questions that you would be delighted to answer if you only could. There is often the temptation, when asked a challenging question, to move into generalities which will sound pretty good, even though you don't know precisely what you are talking about. This is not an ethical practice. Try to tell the truth at all times. When necessary, say "I don't know." The more you respect the work you are doing, the more clearly you will see that it is not well to speak beyond your experience. People do not think you are ignorant simply because you don't know the answer to a question. They appreciate that kind of honesty.

People will ask you what you think about other channels and other groups. Study your responses carefully, to be sure that they are free from judgment. There isn't anything wrong with giving as honest an opinion as you can about someone else's work as long as you remember that each person's work has an unique audience and an unique message which may be far different than your own orientation. If you can remember that variety is not an indication that someone is wrong, your conversation will be well served. Certainly to condemn another group out of hand is unethical. To condemn any channel or group is not advisable. In the first place you could be wrong. In the second place, it is a wrong use of your power. People need to discern for themselves, to choose and discriminate out of their own experience and thought. Spreading your opinions far and wide on other channels, especially if your opinion is negative, is a way to make yourself feel good at the expense of others, which is unethical enough. Add to that the fact that you are tying the questioner to you by your judgmental information, making that person dependent upon you to know what is right for him or her, and you have a thoroughly unethical practice. Please try to avoid it. You'll find it difficult at first. When you have been upset by material someone has produced, it is difficult to avoid condemnation. After some practice you will find the words coming a bit more adroitly, and eventually you will be able to say something honest about other workers in this field without judging.

I have never seen anyone write, in this new age, on the ethics of training new channels. Perhaps it is not yet a common enough practice for there to be a felt need. However, I am making the assumption that a significant number of channels will end up teaching channeling. Apprenticeship is, after all, the oldest form of teaching. As a teacher of new channels, I will share with you some of my feelings, for whatever use they may be to you. You can guess from what has gone before that I do not charge money for this, as I myself was taught freely, and my teacher before me. I also consider the work spiritual in nature and very exacting, and my teaching of it as part of a sacred ministry, sacred to me and sacred to my Creator. I am not, however, saying it is unethical to charge money for teaching; if your financial circumstances do not allow you to live comfortably without charging something, by all means do so. Just be sure it is a reasonable amount. The ethics of some groups which charge a very large amount to teach what they have to share are to my mind questionable. There is always the argument that people will not use what they have learned unless they pay for it. In the American materialistic culture this is sometimes the case. The theory further goes that if you pay a great deal for something you will pay a great deal of attention to that something. This may also be the case, but if you are doing that, try to make your contribution very, very special. I do not have an avoidance towards money, but only towards greed.

There are two main categories of students: curious and committed. The curious will almost surely not continue channeling after having learned the technique. That's fine. There is nothing unethical about sharing the experience of channeling with someone else who is not dedicated to performing it as a service. You are performing a service to that person in giving the person information. It is well if you are convinced that the person's curiosity is a legitimate one, and not prurient or excessively shallow. That person may have another area towards which he is moving and in which he can be of far more service than he could be by channeling. There are many, many ways to be of service and vocal channeling is only one. Therefore, I do not turn down the curious merely because they do not have an ultimate commitment to using their ability to channel in the service of vocal channeling. As long as there is a fundamental commitment to the spiritual path and a dedication to the service of others the necessary ingredients are present for teaching to begin.

Those whose curiosity is blank and devoid of any metaphysical basis are a category of student it has not proven worthwhile to me in the past to teach. The experience remains empty since the seeker has no previous experience of seeking and finding to form a basis for this experience of learning to channel. And so without any ethical or moral load on it, the experience vanishes like smoke, as do all neutral experiences. That category of student I do not feel inclined to teach, and it will improve your temper to use similar discrimination.

The committed student, of course, is a joy and a delight, and I hope that you get many of them during the time that you serve in this fashion. To these students you have the responsibility of remaining a teacher to them for as long as you both shall live, as this is not a relationship which ends except by death. You may not have heard from a student for many years but if you have taught a person, when he or she writes or calls and needs to pick your brains or your heart on some matter related to your teaching it is unethical to avoid that responsibility.

You will notice that I have not anywhere in this book said a word about the mechanics of channeling. It is not difficult to explain or to teach this technique, but I hope that as teachers you will keep the technique to yourself except within the confines of private instruction with selected students. It's the great numbers of people who are channeling these days, taught in a most unethical manner, and set free upon the world with no one to call if they get into trouble, that prompted me to write this volume. There is a reason for the word occult; it means hidden, and some things are just better hidden. The keys to the invisible world are hidden because they are invisible, and should remain so because that's part of the nature of inner work. To take this kind of key and put it before a world which is an unpolarized amalgamation of positive and negative souls is to cast pearls before swine. Better teachers than I have been against that! This chapter will probably be longer if the book is printed again, because I expect a lot of questions from readers on the ethics of channeling simply because the field is relatively new and for the most part completely ungoverned. We dwell in the lacuna between the seen and the unseen worlds, and laws are either civil, to deal with seen things, or religious. Since we do not accept doctrine or dogma in the same way that a church does, no body of religious persons can control us. Since it is not against the law to speak or to print and distribute one's writings, the civil courts have no real way to control our activities. We must control them ourselves. I hope you will think ethically and behave ethically for it will affect not only the personal ease with which you are able to live your life, but will also shine through in your channeling work.

Chapter Nine
Holding Meditations

When I was contemplating what I wanted to convey on the subject of holding meetings, I realized that a lot of the savvy that goes into being a good group leader cannot be fully covered in any informational book, no matter how detailed, because people are infinitely various and each person will present unique and sometimes novel problems and challenges. The suggestions that follow are an attempt to regularize some of the more common challenges and come up with pointers that more than one or two of you may find useful.

People are creatures of habit and it will take them a while to get used to setting aside the time for your meetings so that they will be free to attend. For the first month, expect people to find it a little difficult to remember just when you do meet. Consequently, if you are only willing to hold a month or six weeks of meetings you will probably not build up a group of people that is committed to meeting and working together on spiritual questions, unless the group has a strong affinity, as sometimes does happen quite rapidly.

Once you have made the commitment to have a group and have decided on the day and time, whether it is weekly, monthly or fortnightly, pay close attention to your stability. If you see something coming up in the future that you absolutely cannot avoid, get a substitute to hold the meeting for you if at all possible. Just one week of being without a meeting can throw people off. They stop coming and perhaps never get the habit again once you are back. Remember that they are not in the business of serving you by accommodating unusual schedules that you might find convenient. You are offering a service to others and hopefully you will want to do so at others' convenience. This is not to say that you must hold meetings on a Saturday night because a member asks you to do so. If that is your night to spend personal time alone or to celebrate or coze with friends or family, honor yourself enough to keep private time private. But, once having chosen the time convenient to you, make it as convenient as possible to everyone by being there dependably at every meeting. You will note that I have little advice about the frequency with which you wish to hold your group meetings. I have never found any virtue in a particular periodicity. Weekly meetings are probably more grateful to those who come chiefly for inspiration and meditation. A longer time apart means more time to prepare programs and less time to develop a feeling of community, so channeling groups that are placing an emphasis on study can meet with any periodicity with good results. The first person to consult is, of course, yourself. You're helping far more if you offer fortnightly meetings for years than if you choose a rigorous schedule in a burst of energy, then burn out.

Your program format is entirely up to you. I would suggest that you carefully consider the benefits of evening meetings since more people can come then than at any other time. You would be frustrated if you attempted to keep the social processes out of your group. Expect social time before and after each meeting. Do not frustrate yourself by hoping that people will come on time, start on time or leave as soon as the study or meditation is at an end. Part of the process of seeking the Creator is talking with other people who are doing the same thing. Your best bet is to listen carefully during social times for opportunities to use the time for study. With a little direction a maundering conversation can be turned into a lively discussion. Sharpen your ears and your vocabulary and cultivate the flexibility that it takes to use interesting concepts within an aimless conversation as the starting point for a far more intentionally vectored discussion.

Don't expect people, by and large, to be able to sit longer than ninety minutes. Most people need to stretch after about 45 minutes to an hour. Sometimes this is quite impossible as one is right in the middle of meditation or a speaker's finest words at that point. However, scheduling material upon which one has to concentrate to last longer than an hour and a half at a sitting is not wise. Possible, often done, and sometimes unavoidable, but not wise. After the program's main content is done, try to build in a question-and-answer period. If your group is studying with speakers, ask the speaker to open his speech to questions and answers within the 60 to 90-minute period. If it is a meditation with channeling, encourage your contact to open the meeting to questions. The process of learning almost always involves questions and answers. Learning by rote works well if you have an audience completely under your control and are absolutely sure of what you are saying. If, instead, you feel that what you know is true for yourself but not necessarily so for others and if you wish to give others the free will to search as intensely as you have, you will encourage questions and discrimination in your students and discourage rote learning. If people do not know why they are thinking, saying or doing something it will all get mixed up anyway when the student attempts to put it to the test, so try not to be intolerant of others' confusion but, rather, support and nurture creative confusion and questioning.

If you are having people in your home especially, but even if you are meeting in a public place, you as leader are responsible for refreshments. You may want to take up a collection in order to pay for them. Some study groups charge admission to cover the same costs. I strongly suggest that you offer only beverages before a meeting. Coffee and colas with caffeine are considered helpful for those involved in channeling sessions, since there are some indications that caffeine aids the telepathic process. Afterwards, your hospitality may be as generous as you wish. However, before a quiet, sedentary activity such as sitting in a meeting it is foolish to load people's stomachs up with food, and, heaven forbid, liquor. Both make people feel logy and drowsy, a consciousness antithetical to the questioning process.

Before you begin to have meetings, do some thinking about how you feel about hospitality. Face the responsibilities of what you will require of yourself in order not to feel guilty about offering domestic courtesy and be sure that you can satisfy yourself. I would suggest that you encourage people to help themselves even if it is your own kitchen. Put things out where people can find them fairly easily and let people serve themselves. You will be far more helpful to your students sitting and talking with them than you will be serving them drinks.

You need to be right there listening as much as possible because you are in a position to note, to some degree, the dynamics of the group. You will be hearing things that bring a group together and things that drive a group apart. If you notice that new people are feeling ignored and being left out you can make sure more than anyone else there that the person is brought into the conversation. If you hear joking and kidding you can encourage that and help the group to feel more cohesive and tied together in an enjoyable way. Take this side of being a leader quite seriously. It is most important to people who are finding your group and coming for the first time. It is the community as well as the channeling experience that people want when they come to you. It is human nature to want to belong and many people who are awakening to what may be called a cosmic awareness feel distinctly odd. Your group is one place where an "oddball" with a questing mind and heart can come and not feel very odd, since everyone else in the group is in the same boat. Try to use your personal assets— sexuality, intelligence and personality—to make your group members feel comfortable and at home. Yes, I included sexuality: we all have it and we're all pretty aware of it. I don't mean, ladies and gentlemen, that you should flirt with others and be anything but chaste with one another as a general rule. What I mean is that you may smile warmly at someone and position yourself in a vulnerable and open way, perhaps moving slightly past the usual boundary of social space for a moment or so for the sake of making someone feel like a more intimate friend to you. This is a sexual tactic oftentimes. However, it can be useful to you as a leader in making people feel more comfortable. You are acting in an impersonal role as a group leader and you may look upon all of your assets as being impersonally appropriate as long as you are not charming people with mixed motives. Charm them; make them feel comfortable; but do it without attachment to any outcome, for you do not want to manipulate people. You only want to make it possible for them to feel comfortable. Almost everyone is shy in a new environment, and some people remain shy always. There will be more shy people coming to your meditation group or study group than you will meet in the general run of social intercourse since contemplative, thoughtful people are also often introverted. Expect and be ready for this challenge. If you yourself are shy, as am I, start saying to yourself, "Love the one you're with." It'll help.

If you have meditation students that are learning how to channel from you, try not to yield to the temptation to use your public meetings as teaching meetings for your students. Let the content of the meetings be devoted entirely towards contacts which are intended to inspire those who have come to hear the channeling. The teaching process is time-consuming and much too wasteful of your other students' time to be acceptable for the public meetings. It is also more difficult for new channels to exercise their instruments in front of a larger group of people than they have been used to in the intensive teaching sessions. It is better not to put a new instrument through that until the instrument says to you, "It is time for me to channel in a public meeting."

Here is a list of don'ts for you with a few comments.

Don't throw your weight around. You have developed opinions on everything that you have thought about or at least you are in the process of doing so and can talk about that. Because you are the leader of a group, your students may be hanging on your words. You may find the experience a bit heady and start offering your opinions on everything from the right recipe for Boston clam chowder to the validity of the Shroud of Turin with the same careless grace that you offer your opinion on how to aid one in deepening the meditative state.

Don't do that. The temptation is great. But that is exactly what it is: temptation. As a channel you are the ideal of yourself. You tune yourself to a state that you probably do not enjoy as a private person. When you come out of meditation and are not channeling you and I are as much bozos as anyone in this world. Our opinions matter no more than anyone else's, and someone else may have a better recipe for clam chowder! Don't misuse your influence.

Don't assume that people know anything. We turned the lights out at a very large public meeting years ago and settled down into the muscular silence of eighty seeking people. Into the thick velvet dark came a tentative masculine voice inquiring, "What happens when the lights go out?" We hadn't told this new student what to expect! Talk to your students before their first meeting about how your group meditates, about what channeling sounds like, what conditioning sounds like, what aids there are to meditation and so forth. Be sure that you have explored with the student the basic reasons that brought him or her to the meeting. Don't wait for confidences. Be bold and say "What brings you here tonight?" The sentence or paragraph answering that question will enable you to follow through with the information that that particular student needs for orientation to your particular meeting. No two meetings are alike. No two students are alike.

Don't take the formation of the circle lightly. Don't leave your own circle, and plainly tell anyone else who does so that it is undesirable. Circles that are restless and broken make it very difficult for good channeling to happen because the energy of the group is too unreliable. The energy can be rather low and still be excellent for channeling if it is stable throughout the meeting.

Don't lock your door during a meeting unless you want to make it impossible for late-comers to enter. Nothing is more distracting than a doorbell or knock in the middle of a profound silence or a quiet inspirational channeling. Unplug the telephone also.

Whatever you do to tune the group, don't let it be a spoken relaxation session unless you know each student well enough safely to predict that no one has the slightest probability of going into trance. I have had that happen to me on a couple of occasions. Once, spontaneously, and there is nothing that you can do about that. The other time it was my fault. I did not realize how very susceptible one of my students was to the deeper levels of concentration and effectively hypnotized him into a trance state. All I was doing was telling people to relax their heads, their necks and so forth, moving down to the toes little by little. Everyone else had a very good meditation. But for Charlie it was excruciating. This excellent channel has not used his gift since the time that he had so much trouble getting back into his body as a result of my relaxation suggestions.

Along the same lines it is well for you to call out the name of anyone who does not begin to move after a meditation. If anyone in the circle is sitting absolutely still, leave the lights off and be sure that the person is responding to his or her name before you illuminate the room. It is physically painful to someone in a trance and out of the body to come back into the body as quickly as one must do when the turned-on light triggers the reflex that pulls the consciousness back into the body.

Don't expect your students to attend meetings regularly in *perpetuo*. Some will stay a month, some a year; many curiosity-seekers leave after their first meeting never to return and a tiny few will eventually offer to join your work, becoming colleagues and associates. Know that a student will have an internal rhythm and needs to come and go in freedom. Avoid in every possible way making people feel guilty about missing a meeting, and don't assume students are ill because they miss a meditation. Your serene refusal to be egoically involved in who comes to meetings makes it possible for old-timers to dip back into the old group when the desire arises.

Don't get upset if a batch of new people suddenly falls in love, messily, with each other. The experience of opening the heart chakra to unconditional love is powerful, and if it happens to several people at once they may well believe that the whole world is full of wonderful, adorable people, especially the other students so similarly enthused. Counsel caution; keep and honor any confidences and trust that time will sort out the lovebirds into metaphysically and socially appropriate pairings, plus "leftovers," single people who are quite benefited from exposure to universal love, and usually more fit than before for a deep relationship.

Don't assume that you will remember anything. This last may be my private taboo, based upon my "spaciness." I make absentminded professors look smart. However, it may well be that to some degree we all have faulty memory. Get new students' addresses and phone numbers as soon as you can remember to do so. We use a Guest Book. There may be some reason that you want to call someone up on the phone. You will have a precious hard time doing so without a complete list of your members.

Try to record all of your channelings or your speaker's talks if you have any thought at all of keeping an archive of what you have done in this endeavor, or if you contemplate publishing your material. I found out years ago that no matter how obvious it may be to you that this particular session is not going to be worth recording, it will be *that* session that you did not record that you will wish that you had recorded.

Write down all the things that are borrowed from you, assuming that you are holding the meetings in your home and that your library is open for browsing. It is almost impossible to remember to whom you have lent books or other materials or when you lent them. If it is all written down at the time a book is taken it is much easier to retrieve the volumes that you have spent some resources to collect.

There are some do's to meetings as well, in my opinion.

Do try to keep it light. There is nothing more serious than the search for truth and yet there is a tremendous amount of humor involved in the nature and details of our quests. Much about the human condition is quite ridiculous and to put on the cloak of unflappable dignity is to leave a good deal of human nature quite uncovered. If you feel that the group is getting overly serious, or if there is some special occasion, by all means have a party in which no one has to say a single serious thing or listen to serious words. A silent meditation is almost always welcome, but in a party atmosphere it is not always necessary. In a serious-minded group it is good once in a while to get together just to laugh.

Do stay on good terms with your opposite numbers whether they be local or far-flung. Try to respect and have fellow feeling for people who run other groups. If someone is holding a meeting at a particular time, take pains yourself to choose another time, or talk to the first group about finding some way to accommodate each other so that both groups can appeal to the same people. It is a very large city indeed that has an unlimited supply of metaphysical seekers.

Do tell your story. Let people know how you got started in channeling and how you came to be offering group meetings. Nothing makes a person feel more at home than the feeling that he knows you. And nothing makes a person feel closer to you than knowing your story. In this particular application it is not egoistic to talk about yourself but a necessary part of being a good leader.

Note: anything can be overdone!

And, finally, do talk a lot about the concept of being a light group. There are a lot of people all over the world who share the concept of generating more and more light on planet Earth and who see that planetary generation of love, compassion and peace as being the most important work that we can do. You, as a group leader, need to make people aware that you do not function alone but that there is a large network of light groups in the community of metaphysical seekers, all of whom are dedicated to the same propagation of planetary light to offer to the Creator on behalf of Earth. When Don Elkins, my beloved companion and fellow worker, was alive, he used to "joke" a lot about saving the planet. Don always thought big, and I believe that he affected more people personally than almost anyone else I have ever met by his thoughts, his vision and his very being. It may seem like impossible, idealistic thinking to talk about generating enough light to create a different Earth. But that is the direction in which light groups tend to move. The more deeply one thinks about the reasons for banding together in groups, the more one realizes that the formation of any group that is positive in polarity is based upon the theory that we all are one and that together we are more powerful and able to aid others than we are separately. This makes other light groups most precious to us.

Above all, see yourself as ministering to people seeking truth. Your group is most likely made up of people who would go to some church, be it Christian or non-Christian, if only they could deal with the doctrines and dogmas of orthodox religion. Your group is functionally a kind of church, which is a good thing if you can respect the concept of group worship without insisting that to a general reverence be added specific detailed beliefs which your people are not able to accommodate. Respect your group as if you were a priest and they were your congregation. You are in the role of teacher to earnest pilgrims seeking the truth. You are ill-suited to lead them. Everyone is. Don't let that stop you from trying but rather keep a merry heart, a light touch and a warm smile as well. Balance every instinct towards compassion with a careful examination of the direction of conversation so that you do not offer sympathy when it would be more instructive and helpful to put things in perspective for a student. Always err on the side of compassion, but let your experience guide you and when you feel that a person is too close to his problem, do not be afraid to use your position as teacher to get the student's attention and say not "I know what is right," but rather, "Here is something to think about."

Good luck with your group! My prayers are with everyone who undertakes this appreciated and most needed service.

CHAPTER TEN
OFFERING WORKSHOPS AND SEMINARS

Like holding meetings, offering extended programs is impossible to cover fully in one chapter. But some generalities hold pretty true. Here are some pointers to help you put a class or weekend study program together if you find yourself wanting to offer more than a meditation meeting.

A workshop is not a spontaneous event but a planned process. Production of a weekend is and should be rather extended since there are a good many factors that go into a smoothly-running workshop. The first question you want to ask yourself when contemplating a weekend study program is, "What body of material or what concept do I wish to express, discuss and study within the framework of this seminar?" This may sound simplistic. However, many a seminar has foundered on the rocks of muddled planning because, regardless of how well-produced the seminar was, the program did not have a cohesion that made it readily assimilable by the students. You need to decide just what material you want to cover. Remember that most programs are too rich rather than too poor. In an intensive workshop setting with all of the resources which a group of like-minded people represent to each other available, the amount of material that can be digested is still rather small. Any idea that needs to be manipulated by the students needs not only discussion time but also free time, free in the sense that there is nothing scheduled. You can count on your students' finding people with whom they are especially compatible and talking with them if you give them the chance and a little encouragement. A great deal of the useful work in a seminar takes place in the so-called free time.

If you have not presented this seminar before, practice your presentations. This is tremendously different from my advice to the holder of a meditation meeting, for I believe that meditation meetings need to be left largely spontaneous. One certainly cannot plan ahead what subjects will be covered and so forth unless one is in possession of an extremely accommodating contact. However, the points that seem so easily made when one is thinking out what one will say do not retain their chiseled architecture of logic when subjected to the pressures of many people looking expectantly toward you for words of enlightenment. Nothing will stand you in as good stead as honest rehearsal. If you are not satisfied with what you see when you talk to yourself in the mirror, practice again. You will find when you actually give your presentation that it is quite a bit different, probably, from what you have practiced at any time in the past. Nevertheless the confidence that you feel because you have practiced will be invaluable to you.

The reason seminars work so beautifully in focusing people's attention is the "birds of a feather flock together" law of common interest: mutual interests make for excellent communication. You are, in addition to presenting a certain kind of material, responsible for overseeing an environment in which that material can be best put to use during the time in which you are offering it. You have no control over where your students will go when they finish your seminar. While they are with you, however, it is well to be painstaking in your attempts to produce not only a good program but a good community environment for allowing that program to do its work. The number of details that must be attended to mitigate against setting up a workshop hurriedly. It is far better to begin early in your planning.

The first consideration is where the seminar shall be held. If you are holding it in your home, you will be involved with one set of circumstances, if in a motel or other public lodging place, you will deal with another. Assuming that a majority of people will choose to hold their seminars in a public meeting place, let's look first at the advantages and disadvantages of that arrangement. It is a great advantage to have everyone under one roof. This can happen in a home or in a hotel. It is, however, likelier to happen in a hotel since most of us do not have homes which lend themselves to accommodating sizable numbers of guests easily. In the public situation the meals are available from the hotel's restaurant and all of the details having to do with the safety needs of the people in your seminar will probably be taken care of by the management. If you have decided to have the seminar either in your own home or in a natural outdoor setting you are facing all of the production yourself, possibly with the assistance of the people in your seminar. If you are responsible for all of the details you need to start quite a bit ahead of time in nailing down your place of meeting, wherever it may be and, once it is reserved, in making quite sure that everything is laid on for the smooth running of the seminar schedule.

In a home or natural situation, shall you ask your students to cook their own food? If so, you need a carefully made schedule giving everyone his or her fair share of the work. Shall you hire a caterer? If so, you need to determine that expense and be sure that it is covered either by funds that you already have or by monies sent in by the participants in the workshop. No matter who's cooking the food, if you are responsible for the food it is a good idea for you to make out menus carefully before you go shopping. Plan simple foods but hearty ones for people are ravenously hungry at seminars and grow extremely restive when the food is scant in supply or too fancy or different to appeal to a relatively low common denominator of taste. This is not to say that you need to plan hot dogs and hamburgers as your food. You may be a vegetarian and find such foods intolerable. Whatever food that you plan to fix, try to keep to the middle of the road in your selections of what to fix. Think of the food not only for its basic food value but for how much enjoyment it will give in the eating of it. Details of this kind are most appreciated during a seminar. Once you have your menus made, purchase all of your groceries that can be bought ahead. There are always last-minute purchases that are necessary but the more that you do ahead of time, the less that you will have to worry about once the clock starts rolling on your seminar.

Know where you are going to hold the seminar before you advertise it for the first time. The number of students that you can accept depends very much on the adequacies of whatever place that you have chosen as the seminar setting. Don't accept extra people just because you feel sympathetic towards them and want to include everyone that wants to come to your program. There can always be a next time. Accept only the number that can be housed comfortably in the location that you have chosen. Overcrowding a seminar in order to be of more service or in order to make the seminar more lucrative is counterproductive in that an overcrowded situation makes everyone uncomfortable and diminishes the effectiveness of the seminar.

Once you have accepted the number of people that you can house, figure out how all of them are arriving. Let these people become three-dimensional to you at this point rather than having them remain names on a piece of paper. Some will be coming in by car. However, unless you live in a very large metropolitan area and have only advertised locally you will probably be meeting some airplanes in order to collect your people. Either you or someone in your organization needs to be of whatever service you can to each student as he arrives. It is usually possible to make some kind of arrangement to retrieve everybody. If you run into a snag because you are picking up too many different people at too many different places, don't worry because you are inconveniencing someone. If you were not making that person wait for you to come pick him up that same person would have to get a cab in order to come to your house. Indeed, some may wish to do that and spare both of you any inconvenience. However, it is quite normal for people to be willing to put up with a certain amount of inconvenience in order to have a few moments alone to chat with someone who is on the seminar staff, prior to meeting everyone. There is always that feeling of butterflies in the stomach before the students meet each other and the ice gets broken.

Be sure that you have planned adequately for sleeping arrangements. Have a space on your application sheet for students' special needs. I, for instance, travel with my hot pad, a three-in-one plug and an extension cord. None of these things is a lot of help to me if there is no electricity. There are other accommodations that I make because of having arthritis and I do not think that I am much different from other people—each of us has certain special needs. Sometimes these needs are pretty important. Be sure that you have arranged not only for sleeping quarters for everyone but for the special needs of special people. If you do not have maid service you will need to run through the same process that you did with food: you will need to decide if you wish to do it yourself, hire someone to do it for you or engage all of the community of students in a clean-up routine of some kind. Whatever your decision is, be sure it is well in hand when the seminar opens. If you are scheduling students for KP and cleanup be sure that they have that information before they sign up for the seminar. Some truths are best told at once!

The creation of a good environment for seating the information that you are offering during this seminar is enhanced by certain tried and true ice-breaking methods which add to the social bonhomie of the people involved. Try to have a sing-along complete with song sheets, if necessary, at some point during any seminar regardless of how likely it would seem that music would be a great spiritual aid. It makes people feel good to sing together, especially songs that they are fond of. Get out your old Beatles song books and other "classic" rock and popular songs as well as some of the favorite spiritual tunes that you may want to share. Marshmallows or corn and potato roastings are nice accompaniment to a crackling bonfire around which the singers may sit. Almost every group has a guitarist in it so be sure to ask your students to bring their instruments with them. Parlor games such as charades are excellent, and other good icebreakers like shifting table assignments, joke-telling periods, common exercise periods and one-to-one sessions will occur to you as well as ideas which will come out of your own information and style of hospitality. Just remember that you are the head of a very real family for the length of time that the workshop is going on. Treat it lovingly. Try to avoid unfortunate legal problems even if morally you are not against a specific drug's use, by requesting that there be no drugs other than prescription drugs used on your premises. And with that parental discipline out of the way, try to let your guidance be benign and creative.

In order to be thorough you need to have nailed down the place that you are going to use for the workshop setting four to five months ahead of time if you plan on attracting people to your seminar by advertising. Most publications close their issues to advertisers about two months before the issue is actually scheduled to be published. Since you want to have your ad out six to eight weeks ahead of the time you plan on having the workshop, even figuring conservatively, you need to be quite thorough in your deliberations. Try to keep your advertising honest. Don't exaggerate or defend what you are attempting to teach. You are only offering information. Not only is there no way to defend yourself or your opinions, each person's reality being subjectively determined, it is also unnecessary. People tend to be drawn to what will help them by a kind of inspired hunch and if you offer a workshop you will find yourself meeting people that you seem to have known all of your life. The amazing thing to me is that we do not become more and more aware of how intentional it usually is when we happen to meet people. Sometimes you meet and talk with some new person and are left wondering why you attracted that particular person and conversation. Usually there is something either to work out for the student or between you, or to celebrate as do friends who have not seen each other for a long time. That is perhaps one of the best things about seminars in general.

The care that you take with your paperwork will stand you in extremely good stead. Nothing strains relations between seminar givers and seminar students more quickly than an inadequate supply of informative paper. You should have a complete schedule for every student, not just a schedule of activities, but a breakdown of all of the time that is to be spent including free time, social time and shopping time. Literature about what the seminar is going to address is very helpful to students. If you have a speaker or speakers, offer pictures if possible, names and vitae. List the books which your students are going to need or with which it might help them to be conversant and be sure that they have that list well before they arrive at the seminar. If there is any doubt in your mind at all about the need for literature written especially for the workshop, please do go ahead and commit to paper what you wonder if you need. Many workshops are marvelously full of content but somehow more difficult to digest because there is not one keynote introduction either given by you verbally or offered by you in the form of a written introduction to your students which links each of the speakers and subjects into a common chain of reasoning or unified body with perhaps many details but one overriding theme.

If it is possible it would be well for any seminar to have a supply of paper, pens, pencils, a typewriter and if you have one, a personal computer. Many people learn by writing their feelings down either in a journal or in the process of writing a letter to someone. That kind of creative endeavor is always to be encouraged, and if you can provide plenty of materials and a quiet place to work, your thoughtfulness will undoubtedly be appreciated. Another good resource for you to have is a comprehensive, probably hand-drawn map of the local area showing mileages to your location, where the seminar is and where everything in the community that will be needed is in relation to it. A good resource map would include the nearest grocery, drug store, cleaner, laundromat, shopping center and a nice sprinkling of churches and synagogues if you are holding the seminar over a weekend and intend to provide for those who wish to attend services. Restaurants and movies should be added if people are going to be having free meal times or are going to be responsible for their own meals, or if there will be free time enough for people to go see a movie. You will want to have a complete first aid kit on hand. If you are working out of a hotel it is most likely that details like this are covered. The same goes for smoke alarms and fire extinguishers, a good supply of candies and matches or flashlights and batteries and at least one good, portable radio in case of an emergency. You always think to yourself when you are caught without power, "I wish that I had prepared for this." The time for you to think that thought is not when you are responsible for a seminar full of students. Try to think this one ahead of time!

If you are having your seminar in a pleasant place which offers access to other kinds of recreational enjoyment like golfing, swimming, sailing, horseback riding or just looking at the scenery, you will have to make some decision about spouses, children and pets. I have a personal prejudice against including non-seminar people in seminar-rented rooms simply because the presence of the non-studying spouse or child will distract the seminar student continually.

Perhaps what makes a great seminar more than anything else is you. Know what you are there for. Ask yourself what your forte is and go with it. If you want to have a speaker besides yourself select a speaker whose point of view either compares or contrasts with yours in such a way as to tie together an overriding and unifying theme, and make the connection in your literature.

During the seminar keep remembering what you are there for. Long before the seminar's over you will have become very tired. Try not to let this disturb your focus. You need to be there all of the way. Unless you are a compulsive person, try to give all of your energy to the seminar during the time that you are meeting. Whatever you give, it cannot be too much, unless you have a compulsive streak. Making yourself sick with exertion cannot possibly help a seminar. But if you find your enthusiasm flagging, cast your mind back as many times as needed to the memory of just why you wanted to give the seminar.

In the end, you will need to trust your planning and the incredible gifts which your students will bring with them. If your ideas are sound and your presentation of them good, and if your agenda leaves room for inspiration to flow and for people to talk to each other, you will find that your enthusiasm begets enthusiasm in your students and your love for truth and the seeking process will be answered by the tremendous creative love your students bring to the same endeavor. What you will be creating will, in the end, no longer be your own but will be all of the participants' mutual gift to the Creator. Allow that gift to flower naturally, given the garden you have made, the seeds you have planted. Trust in your students and the learning process.

CHAPTER ELEVEN
CHANNELING AND CHRISTIANITY

We live in a Judeo-Christian culture, and new-age channels need to deal at some point with orthodox religion, as it does not hesitate to deal with you! I am a Christian because of living in the Christian world as well as in the new-age context. I have had, over a period of time, a fairly extensive personal odyssey which I share in part with you in the hopes that my observations may be helpful.

The conservative Christian viewpoint on channeling is that it is a Satanic practice designed to deceive sinners and cause them to fall deeper into sin. The fundamentalist remembers that one should not "suffer a witch to live" and considers anyone who exhibits channeling ability a false prophet. Despite repeated Biblical assurances that the Holy Spirit, a part of the Christed deity Itself, will be with us always, conservative Christians believe that inspired Christian writing began and ended with those works that are now collected into that document that is called the Holy Bible. Consequently, when fundamental Christians attack you it is not because of what channeling is or because of what you are but because of what channeling is not, and what they feel you could never be. The experience of being chided by someone you know is a painful one. When the critic is someone you love, the pain increases. When you are feeling ambivalent yourself about Christianity and channeling you are in the worst of this kind of pain.

For what it is worth I will share with you my own version of mystical Christianity. It is not a complete telling of my beliefs for I have always tried to keep the factual content of my beliefs to a minimum. The purer and simpler the flame of my adoration burns the more acceptable do I find my own religious stance. So what I am sharing with you borders on the naive and simplistic. However, to a mystic there is often a lack of vivid complexity and detail, overmatched by the burst of pure feeling which such a bent of mind offers one.

I believe in a mystery. I believe in one God. I believe in one truth, one Logos, one consciousness in all of creation. I believe in that which is behind all which we have ever thought and everything we see. Many are the ways in which the world of facts and figures, of writing and calculating, is made available to us. However, no matter how many ways that you name, ratiocination offers us only ignorance of ultimate cause and so aids in the discovery of mystery. There are no ultimate answers which the rational mind and all of its endeavors so far recorded in written history on this planet have offered to any of us.

It is logical to me that there is an ultimate and noumenal answer, source and Creator. I am unable to conceive of the creation's being as orderly as a timepiece and productive of so much beauty of thought, word, intention and deed and then to believe that there is no Creator. Therefore, I choose to worship the Creator that I cannot see and will never fully know in this life. I worship the mystery which I know is there.

It has been my observation in over forty years of incarnation that the universe is incredibly kind. We are such vulnerable creatures, yet somehow for every problem there seems, eventually, to be a solution. Thus I am given the clue that the nature of my Creator is a loving one and that its acts towards me have been supportive. Or, to put it another way, its acts towards the creation of which I am a part are supportive. The creation witnesses to the Creator's redemption. I am fascinated by the grandeur of all that there is and I seek to know the truth about it, knowing that every time I come closer to the mystery, the mystery will remove itself from me once again, so that no matter how much I learn about the Creator there will be an infinite amount more that I do not know. Behind all theological assertion and discussion is the unity in which I believe. Behind my religion or any other I see the same Creator.

I was born with the gift of faith, in my case the gift of love for Jesus Christ. With this amazingly powerful gift already mine it was up to me only to commit myself, as I advised each of you to do, to one carefully chosen way of living a life in faith. My choice of Christianity was logical and, of course, a sentimental favorite, from my point of view. If you have an attraction to Christianity, yet some things about it cause you to question your desire to declare yourself Christ's own, I urge you to begin talking with someone who is sympathetic both to Christianity and to your gifts.

I believe in the Christhood of Jesus of Nazareth. His achievement was to live up to his potential and to share it with others. He became part of the consciousness of the Creator of us all, in my belief. His consciousness was truly Christed. In addition to worshipping the Christ in Jesus I love the man about whom I have read. His words in the Bible command my respect, my obedience and my discipleship. Unlike the conservative Christian whose cry is "You can only serve one Lord," my assumption is that no matter what I do I am serving one Lord. I accept Jesus Christ as my personal savior. I perceive the consciousness of Christ as being the articulated consciousness of Love. Love is the nature of the Creator, in my view, and signals to me the presence of redemption in every moment of experience, waiting only for us to celebrate it, turn to it, claim it and move onward from being redeemed from our humanity to redeeming any experience that we meet by our own ability to love and to channel the Creator's love. This is not to say that the things that we do are godlike, but that our actions may more and more be manifestations of a kind of channeling which a life lived in faith makes available to us.

I believe in one Spirit who offers gifts to us in our individual vibratory patterns. Regardless of how this is explained in various sects and religions I do believe in an immanent and creative Spirit which is a portion of the Creator and which is in a personal and potentially intimate relationship with each of us.

It is not as important to me to explain my faith as it is for me to live by faith. Consequently, although I read the Bible daily as part of my Christian practice and give substance to what men of inspiration and scholarly achievement can tell me about scripture, I assume that if it does not make sense to me it is because I am taking the words too narrowly or too literally, or have not lived long enough yet. Because spiritual matters revolve around mystery and infinite values, it is almost impossible for us to expect any rational understanding of faith, and yet the act of living by faith is one of the few available whole-hearted responses of a person of integrity to the realization that we do not know anything. Many facets of Jesus' life and ministry which are hard to believe because of extraneous detail can cogently be grasped as allegories. For instance, I am basically indifferent as to whether Mary was a virgin when she conceived Jesus. Historically, this is not an important part of my love for Jesus or my worship of the deity of God in Christ. Metaphorically, it is very important to me for understanding the birth of my own or anyone's spirit. Mary's act in accepting and celebrating what her Creator asked her to do was an act of pure faith, and so it is for all of us. Our first step in a life of faith is to believe. Mary had to nurture this over many months, "Pondering it in her heart." When our faith is new it must be protected as much as the child must be enwombed in order to live long enough to face the outside world. The birth of Christ, then, may fruitfully be seen as an allegory for the moments and months when your life in faith first comes in contact with a world which is quite often seemingly without faith. It is possible to work one's way through Old and New Testament alike, seeing the infinite possibilities in understanding those things which are deeper than words.

I believe that we are all channels in one way or another. Over a period of years we look at ourselves, notice what things are easy for us and what things difficult. We begin to become aware of the gifts that we have, whether they seem small or great, and as our life proceeds we each decide how to offer our gifts. We ask two separate questions about our gifts. The first is, "What nourishes me?"; the second is, "How can I nourish others?" My answer to the first question is that a life in faith and Jesus Christ nourishes me. The answer to the second question is that I seem to be most helpful serving both within and outside of the established church. I have come to see my channeling not just as an advanced form of meditation, which I was satisfied to call it for years, but also as a kind of ministry offered as sincerely as any orthodox minister but, hopefully, without the weight of narrow judgment to burden my offering of inspiration which is intended to serve not just Christians or non-Christians but anyone who may need the particular information I am able to channel.

It seems only reasonable that a good new-age channel have an excellent chance of having a rather profound spiritual nature prior to becoming a channel. Many of the prophets of history have been religious veterans whose inspired channelings broke new ground for them and for the people that they served, even though they were rooted as persons in a life of faith in a traditional religion.

Views of God change. Perceptions of deity emerge, flourish and vanish. The Creator remains behind all that seems to flash across the stage of our experience, and for me to be channeling seemingly non-Christian spiritual material seems only logical. How could I channel more of what is in the Bible? No word can be taken from or added to that book. What is happening with channels now, I believe, is that because there is a tremendous thirst for spiritual food and drink and, further, because so many people have had bad experiences with the narrowness of orthodox religion, many people now look for inspiration in new-age channelings.

This does not mean that the new-age channelings are right and Christianity, Buddhism, Shintoism or any other-ism is wrong. One version, and then another, of creation's story has come before us. Each version of the truth eliminates some distortions peculiar to older systems of belief and creates new ones. Each re-telling of the way of the pilgrim is, for someone, the clearest path possible to a life in faith and, for others, a path blocked for one reason or another. The function of a channel, as I see it, can be that of adding to the number of ways available to people who wish to work out their perceptions of deity and redemption.

All of the foregoing does not mean that I can take or leave Christianity. Knowing that the ultimate truth is not available to me is, in my mind, no excuse for withholding my faith from the best path that I can find to the Creator. For me, that best path is Christianity, which requires a personal and deeply felt commitment to Jesus Christ. Were I to take refuge in the ultimate view of truth I would certainly be wise, but my possession of a life in faith would be highly precarious. The life of a believer is a continual working out of the details of commitment and I recommend to your consideration all possible efforts to find out what you really think and feel about the Creator of your consciousness and your life so that you can choose your path if you have not already done so and clear your mind to give yourself wholeheartedly to the task of creating a faithful life.

Yes, it is possible to create a life of fidelity and honor, bowing to the ultimate truths of mystery and consciousness and neglecting to worship. But that seems dangerous to me because it is all too easy to get cocky when you feel that you are living a more enlightened life than others. One who acts as *if* he believed in order to reap the ethical and metaphysical benefits of a life in faith will not find himself or herself subject to the numerous and inevitable disciplines which recommend themselves to the active Christian, or the active participant in any religion. One may say that the lack of discipline is a freeing thing, yet I submit to you that in the living of a spiritual life a lack of discipline is a peculiarly killing fault.

If you are investigating any part of new-age spiritual teachings, and especially if you are already a psychic or functioning as a channel, and if you also wish to become or remain Christian, my advice to you is to find a minister who has sympathy for those involved in new-age teachings. I am a member of the Episcopal Church, the American branch of the Anglican communion of churches, sometimes called the Church of England. It has proven to be an extremely helpful way for me to worship because the Anglican Church, historically, fairly bristles with mystics and heterodox members. Its rituals are deeply and rigorously beautiful and magical, yet it is something of an intellectuals' church with a theology that understands the scope, ramifications and near-necessity of doubt. Every priest that I have had since I began my study of meditation and channeling in 1962 has been immediately or eventually supportive of and helpful to me. I have found a strong, caring willingness to hear what I am going through and to support me in what I wish to offer spiritually. The most intense need that I have had of this comes in two parts: the Ra contact and challenges from other Christians.

The unusual circumstances of the Ra contact caused me to pay far more attention to its impact on my spiritual life and its acceptability to the church than I ever paid to any other contact that I have received. The Ra contact information was more specific and more organized and constituted a more nearly complete metaphysical system. Consequently, I was more concerned that my spiritual director read the material carefully and advise me of any spiritually sensed irregularity. My present priest has been most kind in reviewing my material and he continues to keep a wary eye on my activities, for which I am extremely grateful.

He has also been supportive of me when I have been distressed and concerned because of the negative comments of those who fear that I have strayed too far from orthodox Christianity to be considered fully a Christian. If you are an active channel, psychic or new-age person, these concerns will be as difficult for you to answer as they were for me without good counsel. As in any organization, no matter how sophisticated the theology, the church is only as good as the people in the church are on their weakest day. Therefore, it behooves you to choose not only the most appealing church theologically but also the most understanding congregation of ministers and people of that church within the denomination. I could, for instance, go to any number of churches within my diocese whose priests, though of the same faith as my own spiritual director, would be unable to relate to me in any way meaningful to both of us regarding my spiritual gifts.

If a priest is also a mystic he will not need to agree with your mysticism in order to be supportive of it, for he will recognize the living spirit that is also in him or her. If your minister, on the other hand, happens to be one who lives a spiritual life in its narrower sense, finding literal meanings rather than expanded ones for each of the events of the Christian story, then no matter what denomination the minister is in, he probably will not be able to aid you but will be uncomfortable around you. Consequently, if you wish to be both channel and Christian, choose your parish with the utmost care, for it is to one particular community of the body of Christ that you will be committing your faith, your life and your work.

Let me say a word or two about dealing with those who will accuse you of being Satanic. Firstly, do not, under any circumstances, defend yourself. It does not become a pilgrim to be haughty and especially does it not become one who wishes to minister to others by offering the service of channeling. Assume that you will suffer for your faith and let it go at that. If it is important enough to you to remain Christian then it is well to approach the difficulties that you will have in remaining Christian in a Christian manner! Always accept the full measure of criticism and chastisement which your accuser wishes to level at you. If you can avoid listening to it without acting unkindly, by all means do so. But if you are in a situation where someone has your ear and that person chooses to accuse you because of your channeling, then hunker down and listen with compassion and patience. Regardless of any provocation, do not give any offense. Try not to insult people or their beliefs but rather turn your energy towards giving thanks for the caring and concern that caused the person to attempt to help—for that is what accusers think they are doing. Ask your accuser to pray for you. It will almost certainly help you, and it is a very healing thing to make yourself vulnerable to and trusting of someone who seems to be hurting you. Remember that your accuser is a Christian and is trying to live a Christian life just as you are.

If you are not a Christian and you are still concerned with a critic accusing you of being Satanic because that critic is a family member or friend whom you are not able to avoid, I would advise you to follow the directions of the previous paragraph even though you are not a Christian because there is nothing more fruitless than trying to argue with a person about his or her religious beliefs.

Perhaps the greatest caution that I would offer to those who have new-age gifts and desire a life of faith within the Christian church is that you do not need to do anything to "wake up the church." Admittedly the church's ways are a bit rusty and sometimes creak with age, but you will find that any way of practicing the presence of the consciousness of Love looks hide-bound to those who are not experiencing the consciousness of Love in your way. The Christian church is rich in scripture and inspired writing. I have no desire, personally, to add to the Bible for as a vehicle of faith it is wonderfully rich and if I studied every day until I died to my physical body in this life I could not possibly exhaust its helpful depths. It is not true that whereas the church is judgmental and high-toned, wordy or petty, lacking in freedom or Byzantine, new-age religions are free. Any faith confines one as it frees one. Live a life within what you know of new-age wisdom and you will find that you have created your own judgments, rituals, methods, limitations and complexities. Nor is it true that there is a fullness of worship in new-age studies that any orthodox religion lacks. Among the functions of any religious organization are adoration of the Creator and service to humankind. We go to church and/or to meditation to worship and to serve others. We hope to worship with heart and mind wherever we go. As I understand my own religion, there is no fixed boundary between The Church and metaphysical philosophizing. Those who seek hardest in almost any religion can be found reading in many religions, seeking always to enlarge and enrich the view of the mystery which we carry with us and within us.

Within your church, especially if you are in any way responsible for sharing Christian life and worship with others, offer only what you can honestly give in an orthodox way. It is not fair to your church to attempt to bring into play concepts which do not fit comfortably within orthodox Christian doctrine. Of course, if someone asks you privately about a certain facet of the faith and you discover that that person is having difficulties along the same lines that you did when you had to face and blend together the difficulty between orthodox belief and what you yourself felt and experienced as true, then you may share your own path with another. But there is no need for you to complicate someone else's walk with Christ gratuitously.

Nor is there any need for you to attempt to bring those in your meditation group or those for whom you channel to Christ. You may certainly say that you are a Christian when it is relevant to the conversation and you will find that if you declare and witness to your own faith with simple brevity, many people will seek you out and ask you about the Christian walk. It is something that many Americans, anyway, want very much to be a part of because not going to church is, in a way, a separation from much that is good about American life. However, I do not believe in trying to change people, whether it is Christians who will not listen to new-age thinking or new-age metaphysicians who want nothing to do with orthodox Christianity. In either case, it is infringing on free will to offer ideas to people who are not asking to hear them.

A note, to keep myself and you honest. This book, and this chapter, are written "in the garden" of quiet contemplation and composition, and one might think that my walk with Christ never leaves Eden, since I seem to have no visible problems. But, like any intellectual, I am against my own better judgment, frequently gone far into the desert of despair, wandering lost until once again the voice of the Spirit breaks through to me and I am again aware of being redeemed. A life lived in faith does not guarantee what the world thinks of as peace or happiness, nor do one's personality traits cease having disadvantages, if one lives magically. Further, please know that I do not presume to be any sort of Christian apologist, as I have no theological training and speak only as one who knows herself to be irreparably the least of those calling themselves Christian; in no way does my life actually represent my numerous ideals and intentions. Nevertheless, to align oneself with principles of ultimate worth is to greatly enrich, ennoble and simplify a life pattern.

If you wish to write me about Christianity and channeling and the problems that you are having, I would be glad to hear what you have to say and to respond to you.

Chapter Twelve
The Supporting Organization:
Incorporation And Taxation

Forming a supporting organization for channeling done by you or in your group is a frequent response to society's demand for organization, given that your work stabilizes and is productive. Your choices include the legally taxable corporation and the nonlegal, unofficial group. The latter option has the advantage of making it very easy to slide through the system. Until very recently there used to be a disadvantage to this choice in that contributions to unofficial groups, no matter how uplifting their inspiration, had no tax advantage. Beginning in 1987 the tax advantage is greatly lessened because of the changes in Schedule A, Itemized Deductions. This makes running your support group unofficially a more feasible alternative, though you still should keep books, as you will be personally responsible for declaring income.

If you wish to have freedom to do whatever is legal for any corporation to do, you may be interested in forming a legally taxable corporation and paying taxes using corporate tax forms. This would make the business tax-costly, but you could use any asset as you wish, within reason, whereas assets of a non-profit corporation can never become private property.

If one's group has an eleemosynary purpose, it does seem worth the trouble to attempt to get tax recognition of your charitable status. It certainly is some trouble. The IRS needs to be very careful in granting tax letters to 501(c)(3) organizations since the benefits of such standing are many, including not just reprieve from income tax but from sales tax as well, plus savings on mailing rates.

If you choose to incorporate, it is well to seek the advice of a lawyer. This is not to say that a well-intentioned, persistent and patient person cannot eventually learn enough to act as an attorney for the self and create one's own Articles of Incorporation, and then go about the process of applying to the Internal Revenue Service for tax-exempt status. It can be done; I have done it, although not with the formation of the Rock Creek Research & Development Labs., our group's supporting corporation, which has the status of a public charity (The organization whose articles I set up, Eftspan, also obtained public charity status in 1975). There is a lot to know about writing Articles of Incorporation that is not available in any concise form, due to the complexities of state and national laws. Each state has requirements for incorporation, and if you are attempting to write your own Articles, the best beginning is a look at as many other Articles of Incorporation as you can coax other charities to divulge. Since it's illegal to give legal advice to another and since each state has peculiar characteristics, it is impossible for me to aid you if you wish to be your own attorney, except to tell you to be very cautious and careful about what you write. Copy the preferred liquidations clauses word for word, as there are tax code numbers and legal language that could not possibly be created by any amount of psychic intuition or even common sense. Do the same with the closing notary public statement, making sure that the requirements for your state have been fulfilled, and do not consider your work done until your organization's officers have sat down with a notary public and completed a notarized signing of the document. Do not think for a minute that you may take two out of three officers for one signing and the third for a separate one—all signatures must be gotten at the same sitting.

You really are better off if you can possibly afford to find a sympathetic and interested person who is also a lawyer. For one who has been through a lawyer's training, this document is not difficult to frame, and you would be saving yourself a good deal of frustration, as I understand that my experience of having to do everything over at least twice was, if anything, one of the more pleasant experiences available to those who attempt to joust with the world of documents, contracts and government agencies. Actually, my experience with the The Eftspan Foundation, which began in 1974 as a light center near St. Francis, KY., and is at this point more of a wildlife refuge than an active light center, netted me four gloriously beautiful trips through the countryside to our state Capitol, and many an hour of intriguing and fascinating conversation with those I met in the many offices of state government and over the phone with the IRS officers. I enjoyed myself very much throughout the experience. However, for a lawyer, the four trips would have been one, and the frustration level would have been somewhat less!

Whether you become, when you achieve tax-exempt status, a private foundation or a public charity, you will be reporting on Internal Revenue Service Form 990, which, by the way, you have to request from the IRS each year if you have received over a certain amount of donations. That amount is now $25,000 but could change at any time. Actually, the IRS does not ask small organizations with receipts under $25,000 to file 990s, perhaps in an effort to trim away unnecessary paperwork in the light of progressively expensive costs of doing business. However, we have, as a part of the metaphysical principle of absolute honesty and clarity in all relationships, filed one anyway, even in those years when our receipts were under $25,000. Indeed, even if you do not send the form in to the government, it is not a bad idea to fill it out at the end of the year and put it away in a permanent file so that if there is any question in the future, the pertinent facts will be as easy as possible to retrieve. With the advent of computers, this kind of care in record-keeping is far easier to come by, with software to create a tax document each year to be placed in your organization's tax file.

Your basic 501(c)(3) requirement is that monies never return to personal or private use. If you cannot swallow that simple requirement, then you need to stay taxable, whether as an individual or as a corporation. I have known people who are able to put close to 95% of all personal expenditures into the context of one non-profit project or another which is on-going in an eleemosynary organization and, therefore, I know it is possible. However, I don't recommend it for you at all because any gain that you may see due to the relief from personal income taxes is eaten up not only by the metaphysically questionable nature of such account-juggling but also by the amount of time that you must go through in the inevitable IRS questioning. Honesty, at least in my opinion, is always the best policy.

You will need books, a good stout ledger or series of duplicated floppy disc files which will contain certain information which may well be required by the IRS for one reason or another. Ledger books should include:

—list of donations received by contributor, date, and exact amount.

—ledgers for keeping track of assets and liabilities, income and expenses and balance sheets.

—car log, if the organization has an automobile

—appropriate tax forms (990 for a charitable institution).

Archives should include:

—Articles of Incorporation.

—tax letter from IRS which states your official status.

—state annual report.

—minutes of all meetings.

In your bookkeeping, the double entry method seems to be necessary only if you have a more active cash flow than we have ever experienced. If you have a computer, your way of entering data may end up being double entry bookkeeping because of your software, and as long as it is that simple, that's fine, but to keep books that elaborate for a small organization seems unnecessary if it's any extra trouble. You do need some good, sound books, however. Income and expenses can be kept by category. It is by far more productive to keep expenses in the same categories as does the Internal Revenue Service. Those categories include as expenses:

—grants and allocations.

—specific assistance to individuals.

—benefits paid to or for members.

—compensation of officers, members, directors, etc.

—other salaries and wages.

—pension plans.

—other employee benefits.

—payroll taxes.

—professional fund-raising fees.

—accounting fees.

—legal fees.

—supplies.

—telephone.

—postage and shipping.

—occupancy.

—equipment rental and maintenance.

—printing and publication.

—travel.

—conferences, conventions and meetings.

—interest.

—depreciation depletion, etc.

—other expense.

Other expenses that we have experienced in the past are: auto expenses, Xerox copying, advertising, research materials, construction, cost of copyrights, safety deposit box rent and refunds. IRS breaks down income into:

—contributions.

—program service revenue.

—membership dues.

—interest dividends.

—sale of assets.

—fund-raising.

It figures the cost of goods as any other business does, taking gross sales minus the cost of goods equaling profit made. Income categories that show these sub-categories, if applicable, would be well to keep as it will save you trouble at tax time.

The IRS loves balance sheets. There is something warm, fuzzy and incompetent about my mind which I never notice until I look at a balance sheet. One likes to think of one's self as analytical, capable, competent and at least normally able to interpret the written word; balance sheets convince me that I have none of the above virtues but, rather, a head full of cotton wool. However, my personal feelings notwithstanding, a balance sheet is not difficult to fill out, if you have kept the records well and are willing to spend some time talking with the IRS about what some of their phrases might mean. I've worked with several different cohorts on filling out Form 990, part five, the IRS balance sheet, and not one of those with whom I have worked has been able to get through the entire thing without calling to ask questions of the IRS. The same question has never been asked twice! Not knowing what each of your relative weak points might be, I will leave you to it!

You will be receiving a government questionnaire having to do with the purposes of the organization. Our federal government allows for a total of three purposes for an organization and I recommend to you strongly that even if you have only one purpose that you know of, you put down as broad and varied a set of three purposes as you can without being dishonest. The reason for this is the uncertainty of personnel and energy over a long period of time. Had I, for instance, filled out the Eftspan Foundation's purposes as that of research and offering a spiritual or metaphysical center, and left out wildlife preservation, the Eftspan Foundation now would be obliged to report to the government that it was no longer active. This would mean that the land that so many people contributed to would be gone, unless the organization to which Eftspan had decided to donate the land had agreed to allow all Eftspan members free access to it. Because we had the land, the thinking of the Eftspan officers was that we might as well be a wildlife preserve since we all felt that this was an extension of being a light center, with love extended to animals and plants as well as humans. Try to think in terms of the worst scenario when setting up your Articles of Incorporation and stating your purposes.

Also to be avoided in the Articles of Incorporation is being restrictive in the bylaws. Three main functions need to be covered in the by-laws: officers, meetings and members. If you state that your officers will be three, and then later you discover that you wish to add another person to the Board, or perhaps two, you must then notify the IRS and your state of the changes in your bylaws, which means that you must come under the scrutiny of someone who has not previously been familiar with your organization and may have had very disheartening dealings with another charitable organization which was abusing its tax-exempt status. Therefore, write about your Board in as general a language as possible. For instance, if you feel that three is the proper number of officers for your corporation but you would consider any number possible up to nine, write it that way. Write to the limits of your desired room for expansion or contraction.

Similarly, with members, it is least trouble to have no members and simply to take donations. Each thing that you say about requirements for members limits more and more the scope of your organization. It is only necessary to have an annual meeting. Even if you wish to have weekly meetings, it would be better to write the Articles of Incorporation stating only the legal necessity of an annual meeting, the legal minimum for an organization, in order that if you stopped having weekly meetings, deciding to have fortnightly meetings, for instance, you would not have to come under the scrutiny of IRS and state officials over something relatively minor. Use your own judgment, and try to think like a lawyer if you are attempting to be one. Realize that the less restrictive language is, legally speaking, the more freedom you will have within the legal system and try to give yourself as much freedom as you can.

This is not to suggest in any way that you put yourself forward to do anything that is not aboveboard. But you will find—and probably have already found as a private person—that there are situations which one gets into in dealing with an organization of any kind and particularly with the IRS where, with all the good will in the world and with no dishonesty whatsoever, you can and will find yourself in sticky situations. Careful thinking and good record-keeping will be your allies in this area, which is perhaps more alien to a channel than to some people, since there is not a lot of room in a balance sheet for metaphysics.

Do try to keep your sense of humor because the IRS people are not big, bad guys. The tax laws do a very large favor for organizations with nonprofit motives and purposes such as yours, and they are to be appreciated, not cursed. It is easier to do that from afar than when one is in the middle of qualifying for a favorable tax determination or an audit, but try to keep your perspective no matter what. The people there have been uniformly caring and supportive throughout my experience with nonprofit corporations. When you must call the IRS and talk to them about your tax letter or your Form 990—and if you organize, you will make those calls— be sure and pick up the phone expecting to talk to a friend.

There are some things to avoid in setting up your organization. One of them is any accounting method except "cash." Accrual is the other fairly widely used method of accounting, and it does require double entry bookkeeping and considerably more complex record-keeping. For a nonprofit organization, especially a small one, it's just not necessary. In fact any overly complex bookkeeping system is to be avoided. But be sure that you can pull out, by some method of record-keeping, the amount that any one contributor has given within any calendar year as that information is sometimes helpful to the contributor.

If you are selling pamphlets, books or other publications and will have an inventory, try to think ahead and predict when you will have the least amount of inventory. Set up your tax year to coincide with that period so that your inventory-taking will be as easy as possible. Often, one cannot predict one's future inventory with any accuracy, but there are some who publish once a year or periodically and if you fall into that category, do yourself a favor!

Try to avoid simple bad judgment in spending. It is tempting sometimes to want to pay someone who has done so much for an organization, but if you have only enough cash to cover the expenses that you already have, you really can't afford to be paying yourself or anyone else a salary. If someone comes to you with a scheme for getting a lot of contributions for your organization, think carefully about what the ad campaign would cost the organization in relation to the amount of contributions it would generate. Consider, also, the metaphysical appropriateness of the ad campaign. The IRS will pick up on salaries and benefits and on the cost of the campaign. There are whole schedules in the Form 990 having to do with these points. There are some questions there that you want to be able to answer "No" to, unless you have a great deal of money coming in and can truly justify the amounts spent on salary and ad campaigns.

Although I have talked with government agencies about our research in years past, the government has never funded any of our research, nor do I think it likely that they would offer to fund yours! However, it does seem sensible to caution you about having any dealings whatsoever with the government, or, indeed, with any politically-motivated action, especially lobbying. There are many questions on Form 990 having to do with involvement with things political. The practice of channeling is profoundly nonpolitical and it would seem to me best to stay out of that fascinating earthly arena of action.

Lastly, avoid giving anything away if it has salvage value. Junk can, of course, be given to anyone who will take it off, but if it is useful and functional, and you want it, buy it from the organization. Don't just claim it.

For those of you just now beginning to consider writing your Articles of Incorporation, the present record-keeping necessity is great. Most organizations miss keeping proper records at first. Unfortunately, it is your first couple of years' records that the IRS will use to determine your tax status. And that precious tax status letter will be the result of your work at the beginning. Keep records of donors and of all:

—grants.

—contributions.

—membership fees (if you have decided to have members).

—interest.

—dividend income.

—business income (unrelated to your purposes as an organization, generated by a money-making project).

—taxes levied on your behalf (if you are a school).

—services of facilities provided by the government (such as a place to meet).

—and especially a careful record of all expenses (see above checklist).

They will be wanting to find out how much was given by large contributors for each year as well as how much was given in total for each year. Consequently, a card catalogue filing system was the answer that we have come up with, pre-computer, to the question "How will we know how much each person has given?" The advent of the personal computer age means that this information can be kept on disks and retrieved and added to as needed, a vast improvement in the system.

Make sure that you do keep these records, one way or another, and good luck to you as you embark on what may seem at times to be an impossible scheme: the corralling of physical details to support metaphysical seeking. It is an unlikely thing for a mystic or a channel to be doing. Yet it needs to be done. If you are an instrument but find yourself incapable of paper work, I urge you to find yourself some help, for you will find, as unlikely as the combination of paper and metaphysics seems, that the world of paper is not actually out to get the psychic but rather wants to do everything it can to help charitable and lofty causes. Just keep thinking positively, and walk away from a desk that has grown too crowded with a day full of frustration. Books do have the advantage of being utterly nonpsychic. The mistake that you cannot find today will probably show up the next time that you show up at your desk. When in doubt, check your energy level. If you still have plenty, try to remember the last joke that you heard, and plunge back in. If you are running low on energy, patience and smiles, try to remember the last joke that you heard, find yourself unable to remember it, and go do something else that is wonderfully nourishing to heart and soul!

CHAPTER THIRTEEN
PUBLISHING YOUR CHANNELING

Channeling does not exist in a vacuum. Although these latter chapters may seem to have gotten farther and farther away from the heart of what channeling is all about, nevertheless they represent the things that I have found to be concomitant with a responsible approach to the stewardship of channeled materials.

Publishing is not for every channel or for every group. Although your attitude as a channel, for transmission of data, is focused passivity, your attitude as one preparing channeling for any kind of publishing needs to be that of a hard-nosed researcher. Choose only what you consider to be the channel's best work. Note that I did not say choose *your* best work. It is not a good idea for a channel to edit his own material. An objective eye is very helpful, regardless of your point of view as a channel. Some channels do think a lot of themselves. Others think too little of their material and tend to value others' work with less discrimination than their own. Seldom is anyone unbiased about his own work. Whichever way you may be biased, it is well to eliminate the bias by selecting someone who can be relied upon to give good, objective opinions.

When you consider the enormous amount of channeled material, even if you consider only published material and eliminate manuscripts, you are gazing at a repository of millions of words. The attitude of a scientist is appropriate when it comes to publishing because you want to contribute to the field, not merely add look-alikes to already extant material. Wait until you feel that you have accumulated a group of channeled materials of which you can really feel proud.

The range of scale on which you can preserve and publish material is close to infinite. The smallest level is the manuscript, whether it be a holographic copy, which is common to those who employ automatic handwriting or typewriting or tapes. These are unedited and represent an archival record of the channeling work that you have done.

Whether or not you plan to publish at the time that you are conducting a session, do record sessions. If you decide not to use a particular session you have perhaps wasted a tape, but I don't think so. It has been my experience that one often goes back to scan one's older resources when one is working on a project and finds little treasure troves that are most useful. Remember that channeling is some of the hardest work that you will ever do in terms of concentration and emotional and mental care, and it is well not to waste it by failing to employ what the 20th century has in so much abundance—record-keeping devices.

Whether or not you have any publishing ambition at present, then, make plans to begin your own archives. You will need the usual office equipment, most of which is rather specialized and used in libraries. If you do not have a library supply house near you, I recommend that you obtain Gaylord Bros., Inc., mail order catalogue. (Gaylord Bros., Inc., Box 4901, Syracuse, NY. 13221) As a former librarian I can recommend that concern as an excellent and reasonably priced supplier of the various cards, containers, files and so forth that you might need to hold your materials and keep them cool and dry or otherwise preserved.

The next level of care in preservation is creating a transcript archive. Transcripts are much more edit-able than holographs or tapes. You will want to create a standard format for your transcripts if you decide to convert the information on tapes or written by hand to a more easily readable and editable typewritten medium. I recommend that you include the date each tape is made, the names of contacts on the tape, the names of channels used and the names of any questioners whose questions may have prompted answers by the contact through the channel. You may think when you are having a session that you will remember what went on in it, but over a period of years things run together in memory and it becomes impossible to retrieve the knowledge of who, when and where by looking at the tape.

Clean your faithful typewriter—that costs very little—at regular intervals, and keep a good black ribbon in it, for if you do edit your material at a later date, you will want to be able to see the copy.

Also recommended are the use of double-spaced lines and wide margins so that you can write above, below or beside copy during the editing process. It is not always easy to remember just how you are going to cut and paste selections of channeling, and room for notes is often most welcome. It has never been my practice to do more editing in channeled material than is needed to unsplit an infinitive or eliminate channeling errors in transmission, which are usually pointed out quite promptly by the contacts within the channeled message. Sometimes a word is lost and one simply has to guess at the proper word, which I think is quite acceptable if there is enough of a context to go on. The one thing I am not for is changing a channeling or adding to it in any way that has substantive meaning, since the nature of channeled material is that authorship does not reside with the channel. It is not polite to rewrite discarnate entities' inspiring sermonettes! This is so no matter how great the temptation because of the difference in some personally held tenet.

How devastating would it be to you or your group to lose the channeled material that you have produced in the past? If the answer to that is, "Very," you need to set up a safe file, separate from the archive's files, either in a safety deposit box in your bank or at the home of a friend who lives in a distant neighborhood or city. I prefer the latter course since this gives me the opportunity to share the channeling with someone interested in it anyway, as well as to have an archive copy which would survive even a totally devastating fire at my own house.

There are peculiarities to channeling which make setting up a recording system a little challenging. If you or your group's channels have loud, piercing or resonant voices there are no problems that cannot be easily overcome. However, not only do many channels have quiet voices; the nature of channeling is such that it causes many channels to lower what little voice they have in order to flow with the energy which is being transmitted, which is peaceful and serene in many cases. The reason that this can cause problems, by and large, is that most tape recorders are equipped with automatic recording levels programmed into the internals of the machine. There is no way the operator can manually adjust recording volume level. This means that when the machine hears a silent room with one soft voice speaking somewhere in the distance, it turns the level up accordingly to pick up the small voice. This causes a great deal of tape hiss. I am told by the wonderful volunteer (by name, and thank you endlessly, honorable Judy Dunn) who transcribes our Sunday night meditations that the white noise is deafening under those circumstances.

There are solutions. The first is to purchase inexpensive equipment, and we do not exclude the low-priced Radio Shack product which is geared to use with the tie-pin microphone. This type of microphone is excellent and when pinned to a channel's clothing will pick up even a whisper with no problems. Cheap tape recorders do fall apart, and more expensive tape machines do not have the proper-sized jacks for the tie-pin microphones, so the tie-pin mike does not seem to last well, at least not for us. On balance, however, we have had almost as good luck using cheaper equipment as "expensive"! Of course, had we an inordinate amount of funds we would be able to buy *really* expensive, professional recording equipment, both recorders and microphones, which is an entirely different breed of cat from tape recorders on the general consumer market, which are geared far better to play than to record, and could promise one an ideal recording situation. The amount of money that would need to be expended would be beyond most small groups' means. If you have the means, talk to your favorite recording studio engineer or professional sound dealer to find out how best to supply your needs.

The other solution is to get a "better" machine and a very good microphone and hand-hold the microphone when necessary, so that it is always close to a soft-voiced channel or questioner. This involves seating the people in the group carefully. If anyone reading this knows the perfect setup for the inexpensive recording of channeling I invite you to write me and let me know.

The third level, in terms of ambition, of channeling projects is the edited selection of messages on tape or on paper. The likely vehicle for such is the research report or bulletin, put together either like a short newsletter periodically or, if you feel that you have a body of material that is worth publishing as a book, a very inexpensively produced book with a small number of copies ordered. If you decide upon the research report format, you will need to get a masthead composed and a printer. The information on the masthead needs to include the name of your organization, an indication of its tax exempt status and a short declaration of what your group is. Your address should always be included, and if you are in the process of moving or think that you might move within the next few years, you would be well advised to print an address that you are fairly certain will be stable for as many years as possible. Some people use post office boxes and keep them from year to year whether or not they remain in the same place as the post office box. Others use Mom, a friend or a relative. You would be surprised what longevity paper has. You never know when you are going to get a letter from a person who has seen some of your work published years ago and who now wants to read more.

Your choice of a typewriter is personal. Some people are very conscious of the way things look and really are bothered if they do not have a good-looking copy. Others simply don't see the niceties of ink on paper, and concentrate completely on the material itself. If the material is good, they have few complaints about the format, whether or not it deserves it. Most people are not of this latter kind, and if you wish to avoid criticism in the future, you might straighten up your typewriter now! Electronic typewriters give you many special effects that mechanical-action typewriters simply could not unless one had an office-type IBM. Proportional spacing is a good device for achieving a more "printed" look if you are doing camera-ready copy at the typewriter. Some machines, especially computer-assisted ones, allow you to justify the right margin *and* use proportional spacing, which is as good as having copy typeset, if the computer does a good job.

Another format for this level of "just a few copies" of channeling, the modestly printed book, requires that you choose a cover and a title page. Be sure that on the title page you have all the needed information about yourself and your group and on the back of the title page, all the needed addresses, publication data and so forth. Take a look in a mass market book, especially on the reverse side (verso) of the title page, to familiarize yourself with the kind of information that gets put there. Be sure, whether you are choosing the research report or the book as your vehicle, to place the copyright declaration clearly on the title page or on its verso. The declaration should read ©, the copyrighting person or corporation, and the year of publication, all on one line. This protects you even before you have gotten your actual copyright from the Library of Congress. (To copyright your book write: Registrar of Copyright, Library of Congress, Washington, DC 20559 and ask for Form TX.) If you are generating periodical reports you should know that you need to copyright each and every report if you wish to have that information available to nationwide retrieval systems. Books, of course, must also be copyrighted separately. It is a relatively simple task, except for the blanks having to do with authorship. We have copyrighted our channeled material in the name of the contact, not the name of the channel, and the Library of Congress has had precedents for this and allowed it, although the channeling then is classified by the archaic term, "spirit writings," which may not appeal to some channels. There is a faintly surrealistic tone to submitting a copyright to one's government which explains that a book has been written by a discarnate and unborn entity which does not live in the United States, which has done the work "for hire"!

The cheapest binding for a modest book publication—by which I mean, say, under 200 books printed—is the spiral binding. If you use 8½" by 11" paper and type the copy yourself, a spiral-bound volume can be had at a very reasonable price. One note about pricing is that if you wish to tell people how much it costs you to print the book you must figure in mailing expenses and office supplies like envelopes and shipping tape.

The small book or research report can also be put on tape, a medium which many people prefer to the printed word. If you decide to publish in tape form you must put a (p) notice (copyright for recorded material, or "poppyright") on each cassette in order to copyright the material. You would also need to ask for Form SR from the Library of Congress. As with books, that statement on the cassette indicates intention to copyright which makes plagiarism illegal whether or not the Library of Congress has actually received or processed the tape. The same kind of care should go into producing a tape as producing a book. You would not want mistakes and dirty copy in a book, nor do you want garbled language or a noisy tape if you produce in that medium. There are times, however, when if you want to make something available to the public, you must take what you can get. When our research associate, Don Elkins, died in 1984, Jim McCarty and I found that neither one of us had been careful enough about recording and placing in an archive Don's dozens of brilliant and fascinating lectures, given over a thirty-year period. We found that we had only enough material to make one composite tape, 90 percent of which was recorded on a very poor machine with dirty heads in the most unprofessional manner. Our tape machine was probably stuck under my chair. Moreover, a radio station occupied an upper floor of a high rise near the building we were in, and strains of music bled through, drifting on and off the tape with annoying regularity. Professionals could not remove the tape noise or the music, but we felt that it was important to make just one of our Research Director's amazing story-telling sessions available to those who might request it, so we published what we had. Would that I had had this book back when I began this work. You may want to submit your channeled material for magazine publication. It is a small market, but I can recommend the well-produced METAPSYCHOLOGY: THE JOURNAL OF DISCARNATE INTELLIGENCE, (P.O. Box 3295, Charlottesville, VA 22903) as the standard for the field.

The fourth level of publishing scope is the research report or book in quantities over two hundred. I use the figure of two hundred because if you have over 200 pieces of mail to send out at any one time you can save a great deal of money, eventually, by using bulk mailing privileges. When you are sending out a yearly report which has been pre-subscribed, it's very helpful to have the bulk mailing ability. Of course, if you have barely two hundred people on your mailing list it will not pay you to get the permit because it costs a substantial amount of money just to obtain the permit number, and it would be difficult to make up the difference between the savings and the cost involved with the mailing permit.

At this larger scale the instructions given for the more modest efforts become more important—the copyright, the production of a complete masthead and the inclusion of a fairly permanent address. The more books or reports that you publish each time, the more inexpensive each volume is. However, don't be fooled into ordering more copies of the book than you will need simply to get the lower price per volume.

Speaking of money, the binding of a book is a rather large part of the expense of producing it. Although the spiral binding is the least expensive, a staple binding (saddle stitching) is also fairly inexpensive. In that binding method the book is printed on double sheets folded over to make a book with staples at the fold. Perfect binding is more pleasing to the eye and handier for putting one's title on the spine—since the pages are glued together to make a spine—and is correspondingly more expensive. Perfect bindings these days are almost always glued, the cost of stitching being enormously expensive. However, today's glues are excellent, for the most part, so do not feel that you are cutting corners too much if you want to publish a really good-quality book and decide on a glued perfect binding.

At this level you are still doing it yourself. I urge you to stay away from vanity publishers and I say this as a librarian with quite a bit of experience in the matter. They promise you a great deal, all of which is basically true, but almost all of which comes to nothing for 98 percent of their customers. Instead, look for small presses who publish in your field. Often a small press which is publishing a periodical will have quite a bit of time between printing issues and will be glad to have your business. By all means, comparison-shop and put the printer to work who offers you both a reasonable price on the job and a feeling of mutual sympathy over the phone or in person. Printing a book involves a lot of discussion and if you choose a printer who is not easy to talk to, you are not doing yourself any favors. Often the most sympathetic person also offers a good price per job, which helps cut costs. Private printers usually charge half of the cost of printing when they receive a manuscript and half when they deliver the volumes to you. Thus the cost is well-known ahead of time and there are no surprises, unless something occurs right at the moment the process of printing is taking place and you both decide together to make some changes. If you have a printer who makes changes without telling you, use your discretion, but certainly consider going to another printer.

The computer has brought to the home publisher a new ease in typesetting. Formerly the printer had to do that for you. Now, if you have a personal computer which is compatible with your printer's printing computer you can format your book or research report at home on the computer and transmit it to the printer over a telephone modem. The cost to us, at this writing, of typesetting from our publisher, Palmer Publications, Box 296, Amherst, WI 54406, is about ten dollars per page, and if you are printing a book you are talking about a four-figure amount which can be saved by using your computer. Rejoice, if you have one and know how to use it! And certainly if you are considering printing a book which will run 200 pages or more, you might consider getting a computer instead of jobbing out the typesetting, and doing the typesetting yourself. After typesetting those two hundred pages, and thereby making up the two thousand dollars which you have laid out for the computer, you have the typesetting done and a computer left over which can do the same thing for you another time, plus, need I say, a whole lot more.

You will think, after proof-reading your book in galley form, or on the computer, that you have been careful, thorough and complete in your proofing. However, copyreading is an art and not a science. The human eye can scarcely ever be trained to see everything which comes before it. Proofread extensively and redundantly, and after you have finished the process, proofread once more. You will almost always find more errors each time you go through a manuscript.

I mentioned the efficacy of recording the date of every session when you do transcripts. It's also well to preserve these dates in any publication which you may decide to make. It is the only way to retrieve, for a questioning reader, the context of a particular channeling, part of which you may have used in your publication.

Mailing can easily be done from the home, since in most parts of the country there is either a post office very near or a mail carrier who picks up mail at your mailbox. Be sure and get stout envelopes because there is something about a package the size of a book which must distress those who slog through sleet and rain to carry our mail. Until we figured out that we had a problem using bulk rates and services we lost several books entirely. Now we have learned to use clear packing tape and very tough envelopes. Other things that you will need for mailing will be a weight scale, a rate schedule, a zip code book and, if you decide to use bulk mailing privileges, all the rubber bands, stickers and other paraphernalia that the postal service provides free to the permit holder.

Many groups wish to advertise their publications, and a good many of them spend money that they don't need to in order to do so. Spend carefully if you wish to buy advertising. Aim the advertisement at the metaphysical audience to which it will appeal. Use a soft sell, refraining from boasting or sensationalism unless there is a touch of larceny in your soul. Mail-order selling is a science which is very big on hyperbole, and that's fine in a free-market society, but when you are dealing with metaphysics there is an innate morality which I, personally, wish would prevail more often.

If you are going to advertise once in a periodical, advertise at least three times. Studies have shown that advertising is most effective done this way.

Lots of people who have not published previously are probably puzzled by this point in the chapter because I have not mentioned selling your work to a mass-market publisher as an option. I will do so now, but only to discourage you. For every piece of channeled material that gets published by a mass-market publisher there are thousands of manuscripts that are destined to gather rejection slips as easily and inevitably as city snow gathers soot. This is due to the highly speculative venture that any publisher engages upon when he publishes channeled material. If it hits, it hits very well; it if does not hit, it represents an expense to the publisher and most publishers have been stung by channelings which their editors respected and appreciated but which the mass market did not.

One of our books, THE RA MATERIAL, (Originally THE LAW OF ONE in its first private printing) has been published by a mass-market publisher. They did a very good job with it, but it took two years, almost, to get it through the typesetting, proofing and editing process, and even though we do not have to publish it ourselves it is more expensive for us to offer to our readers than any of our other books because the mass-market publisher cannot sell it to us at its cost of printing it and make a profit. We pay the same price that wholesalers do. We have not been lucky enough to have a publisher which wishes to get behind us with promotional tours of lectures or extensive advertising, so we have realized no benefit from mass-market publishing. Consequently, I don't recommend it for your first venture, unless you really don't care about publishing unless someone else can do it for you. In any case I wish you good luck and Godspeed with your work and your materials.

This *Handbook* couldn't be more timely—or more useful.

Channeling is an age-old art, but only recently has it exploded into such widespread popularity that many thousands of individuals are learning how to access wisdom, information, and reassurance from a variety of non-physical sources.

How do you make contact with higher entities who have *your* best interests in mind? And, having done so, how to you retain your sanity and common sense, and develop your humor and humility? If ever there was a manual of channeler's do's and don'ts, either it mildewed away in the mists of time or was incinerated by organized religionists.

Now Carla L. Rueckert—whom we have to thank for channeling *The Ra Material* and *The Law of One*—provides a dandy 20th century replacement. This is a wise, loving, useful book, and must reading for anyone involved in the process of personal spiritual expansion.

Tam Mossman
Editor of *Metapsychology, The Journal of Discarnate Intelligence*

CPSIA information can be obtained
at www.ICGtesting.com
Printed in the USA
LVHW082351300522
720046LV00014B/1195

9 780945 007074